Landscapes of
ALGARVE

a countryside guide
Fifth edition

Brian and Eileen Anderson

SUNFLOWER BOOKS

For Deric and Kate Brown

Fifth edition © 2007
Sunflower Books™
PO Box 36160
London SW7 3WS, UK
www.sunflowerbooks.co.uk

Published in the USA by
Hunter Publishing Inc
130 Campus Drive
Edison, NJ 08818
www.hunterpublishing.com

ISBN 978-1-85691-334-8

Almond tree letter box

Important note to the reader

We have tried to ensure that the descriptions and maps in this book are
error-free at press date. The book will be updated, where necessary,
whenever future printings permit. It will be very helpful for us to receive
your comments (sent in care of the publishers, please) for the updating
of future printings, and for the Update service described on the inside
back cover of the book.

We also rely on those who use this book — especially walkers —
to take along a good supply of common sense when they explore.
Conditions change fairly rapidly in Algarve, and **storm damage or
bulldozing may make a route unsafe at any time**. If the route is not as
we outline it here, and your way ahead is not secure, return to the point
of departure. **Never attempt to complete a tour or walk under
hazardous conditions!** Please read carefully the notes on pages 43 to
52, as well as the introductory comments at the beginning of each tour
and walk (regarding road conditions, equipment, grade, distances and
time, etc). Explore **safely** while at the same time respecting the beauty
of the countryside.

If you would like to offset the carbon dioxide emissions for your trip
to Algarve, go to www.climatecare.org.

Cover photograph: tiled fountain in Estói Palace gardens
Title page: Tiles (azulejos) in Largo 1 de Dezembro, Portimão

Photographs: the authors
Maps: John Underwood, adapted from the 1:50,000 maps of the
    Instituto Geográfico e Cadastral
A CIP catalogue record for this book is available from the British Library.
Printed and bound in England: J H Haynes & Co Ltd

10 9 8 7 6 5 4 3 2 1

● Contents

4   Landscapes of Algarve

Falésia, near Vilamoura

Preface

Legend tells of how a Moorish king married a Scandinavian beauty and brought her to Algarve. She loved to watch the sun's rays seeking out and painting the hilltops in hues of evening gold. But when the summer season faded through autumn into winter, she became deeply unhappy and pined longingly for the snows of her native land. Worried at the unhappy state of his beloved, the king arranged for thousands and thousands of almond trees to be planted throughout the region. Even now, in January and February, the land is dusted with a covering of almond blossom in delicate shades of pink and white lying like a soft fall of snow, filling the hollows and outlining the hillsides.

Below the 'snow' lies a carpet of burnished gold, as the Bermuda buttercups burst into bloom to announce the arrival of spring. Oranges fill the trees; iris, bluebells, and even the insect-mimicking wild orchids follow in abundance. 'Is this the same Algarve', you may ask, 'as the Algarve of high-rise hotels, fine beaches and a coastline so famous that there is no need to look further?' Such is the beauty of the coastline, that few visitors look for more — but we did. We found a countryside full of interest and beauty, quietly awaiting discovery. From flowers and fountains, hilltops and history, to windmills and watermills, we can set your feet wandering to find them all. There are car tours, too, to get you out and about, searching out little-known points of interest — like the huge rose compass *(rosa dos ventos)* on the barren promontory of Sagres, where Prince Henry the Navigator founded his school of navigation, or the Moorish castle and old Roman bridge at Paderne.

But don't think for one moment that we have turned our backs on and ignored the beautiful and rugged western coastline. Wherever it is still unspoilt and free from development, we have incorporated it into a walk. Some of the finest and most picturesque coastline in Algarve is yours to share only with others who are happy to tread the coastal paths. There are quieter bays, too, where you can take a break from walking, for a relaxing dip in the sea and perhaps a refreshing glass of well-chilled *vinho verde* before stepping out to complete the walk.

6   Landscapes of Algarve

Some days are made for relaxing, so why not try a country picnic? We have included a variety of picnic suggestions, many involving only a short walk. Some are set in country villages — like the one at Alte, which gives you a chance to explore an old settlement and enjoy a short stroll by the riverside, before settling down to your picnic lunch. Or perhaps you feel ready for the hustle and bustle of a country market. Here you can feel the excitement of the locals, share the life, the colour, the customs and culture for a few short hours before it all fades to empty stalls.

However you like to spend your holidays, Algarve offers something for everybody. If you like lively resorts or quiet resorts, you'll find them but, best of all, with the help of this book, you can easily escape the crowds. Step out with us and share our delight at finding tranquillity and undreamed-of countryside — in the very heart of Algarve.

Acknowledgements

For this Fourth edition, we would particularly like to thank our good friend Deric Brown of Vila da Luz for the Figueira circuit (Walk 4) and for general on-the-spot checks and suggestions; all the users of the book who send in constructive comments; 'hotter' (tel 0800-468837), who supplied Eileen with the most comfortable pair of light walking boots she has ever worn, ideally suited to Algarve walking, and our ever-patient publisher, Pat Underwood, and her team.

Background reading

Landmark Visitors Guide *Algarve*, by the same authors. For a deeper insight into the Algarvian way of life, track down *Southern Portugal; its people, traditions and wildlife* by John and Madge Measures (published locally; ISBN 972 8262 00 0). Also see www.thetravelmag.com, the authors' online travel magazine.

Praia Dona Ana (near the end of Walk 1)

● Getting about

With so much interest focused on the coastal zone, it is not surprising to find this region is well served by public transport. **Buses** ply back and forth along the main highway, the N125, calling in at the various coastal towns. All the services are timetabled and generally keep good time. It always pays to arrive a few minutes earlier for the bus than the scheduled time. A selection of useful timetables for the EVA bus company (www.eva-bus.com) is given in the timetable section on pages 129-132. The Froto Azul bus company operates in the west (no web site as yet).

There is a very useful **train service** which runs almost the length of Algarve, from Lagos in the west to Vila Real on the eastern border. With 45 stations along this line, it can be a slow journey — taking as long as four and a half hours to travel the whole length, but it is much cheaper than the buses. The full timetable is too long and detailed to include in the timetable section, but a short extract is given, which might be useful for getting to the start of some of the walks. Full timetables are available free of charge from most stations and some tourist information offices.

Taxis are plentiful in the main tourist resorts, and these are especially useful for getting out to some of the more remote regions, but we would advise you only to use official taxis. Meters are not commonly in use, so it is wise to enquire about the fare before you start the journey. In our limited experience, we found that the taxi drivers were fairly consistent in applying the fares, and that we were paying the same rates as the local people. If you can team up with other walkers to reduce the cost, then taxis represent a very convenient way of getting out into the countryside from the main centres but, in most cases, you would need to arrange to be collected to get back again.

The limitations of the public transport system are only fully realised when you want to get out and about into the inland villages and countryside — which you will need to do for many of our walks. This is where a hire car is invaluable. Car hire is relatively cheap in Algarve, much cheaper than in the rest of Portugal, and very popular. See the notes on pages 14-16 about car hire and driving.

● Picnicking

Beaches are popular venues for picnics in Algarve, but there are many lovely and more tranquil country settings. It is not unusual to find small picnic areas as you drive around. These are usually sited amongst trees, with wooden or stone tables and benches.

We have chosen a variety of picnic settings — some along the routes of our walks, others reached during the car tours. Some lie deep in the countryside, others on secluded beaches (but remember that in mid-summer *all* beaches are fairly busy). Most of these picnic spots are easily accessible on foot or by public or private transport. A few, due to their isolation, require more walking — but they are well worth the extra effort involved.

All the information you need to get to these picnic spots is given on the following pages, where *picnic numbers correspond to walk numbers* (the picnics on page 13, prefixed 'CT', are only accessible from the car tours). You can quickly find the general location of the picnic place by looking at the large touring map (on which the area of each walk is outlined in white). We include transport details (🚐: how to get there by bus; 🚗: where to leave your private transport), how long a walk you'll have, and views or setting. Beside the picnic title you'll find a map reference; the exact location of the picnic spot is shown on this *walking map* by the symbol *P* (the best place to leave a car will be indicated, too, by the symbol 🚗). Finally, to help you choose an appealing location, photograph references are given for those picnic suggestions that are illustrated in the book.

Please remember that if more than a few minutes' walking is required, you will need to wear **sensible shoes** and to take a **sunhat** (○ indicates a picnic **in full sun**). A plastic groundsheet or large plastic bags could be useful, especially early in the season when the ground might still be damp or prickly.

If you are travelling to your picnic by bus, refer to the timetables on pages 129-132, but remember — it's always a good idea to get up-to-date timetable information from the bus station or tourist information office.

If you are travelling to your picnic by hired car, be extra vigilant off the main roads: children, animals and adults are often in the village streets. Be careful where you park, too — don't damage the vegetation and flowers, and be sure not to block a road or track.

Picnic food suggestions are not much of a problem in Algarve, where there are well-stocked modern supermarkets. Portimão, Albufeira, Faro and Olhão also boast large supermarkets with their own bakeries and butchers, where you can buy fresh bread, even on a Sunday. Locate the local bakery for a wide choice of fresh bread: *pão seco* (small bread rolls) are ideal for picnics. From the local market buy fresh *pepino* (cucumber), *tomates* (tomatoes), *alface* (lettuce), *pimentos* (peppers), *azeitonas* (olives: *verdes* = green, *pretas* = black), *iogurte* (yogurt), *mel* (honey), *queijo fresco* (very mild fresh goat's cheese), and a variety of fresh fruit depending on the season. There is a good variety of cheeses, cheese slices and portions.

Portuguese specialities, which can be bought ready-made from the delicatessen counter, include *rissois* (rissoles) and croquettes. There is a choice of cooked meats and sausages. *Carne* = meat, usually *porco* (pork) or *carneiro* (lamb). *Peru* (turkey) and *frango* (chicken) are also popular. We also discovered small tins of sardine pâté, ideal for picnics ... but be careful not to buy the 'piquant' variety, unless you like it hot. There is a varied selection of *bolos* (cakes), since cake and coffee play an important part in everyday Portuguese life. Food signs are not usually in English, so it helps to have a phrase-book handy.

Last, but not least, don't forget something to drink. There is a wide range of soft drinks including fruit juice, flavoured yogurt drinks, and bottled water. For more heady refreshment, take a bottle of *vinho* (wine). Portugal offers a wide range of wines, and an enjoyable element of your holiday will probably be trying many of them. *Vinho verde* ('green wine', but usually white and slightly sparkling) is an excellent choice for picnics, but a rosé or light fruity red would be equally acceptable. *Saúde!*

---

1 LUZ — OBELISK (map pages 54-55) ○

🚗 by car or taxi: 20min on foot. Park in the car park at Praia da Luz and follow the notes for Walk 1.

🚌 by bus: 25min on foot. Bus from Lagos to Luz (Timetable 1); alight in the main square. Head down to the seafront and follow it left to the car park (5min); then pick up notes for Walk 1.

It is a steep but short climb to this good vantage point offering excellent views, but no shade.

3a CABANAS VELHAS (map pages 60-61) ○

🚗 by car or taxi: no walking. Park at Cabanas Velhas, at the back of the inlet on the left, 2km along the road west from Burgau.
🚌 by bus: 35min on foot. Bus from Lagos to Burgau (Timetable 1); then follow the notes for Walk 3.
Large expanse of sandy beach, round to the left at the mouth of the inlet, beneath the cliffs. Little shade. Cafe/bar

This spectacular beach, on the route of Walk 10, lies between the settings for Picnics 10a and 10b.

3b ISOLATED FORT (map pages 60-61; photograph page 63) ○

🚗 by car or taxi: 15min on foot. Park as in 3a above, then follow the notes for Walk 3 from the 35min-point.
🚌 by bus: 50min on foot. Bus as for 3a above, then follow the notes for Walk 3 to the 50min-point.
A secluded spot on the edge of the cliffs. Some shade from the fort walls.

3c BOCA DO RIO (map pages 60-61; photographs pages 63, 64) ○

🚗 by car or taxi: no walking, or up to 27min on foot. Either drive direct to the bay or park as for 3a above, then follow the notes for Walk 3 from the 35min-point. Alternatively, park in the centre of Salema and use the map to walk to Boca do Rio.
🚌 by bus: 27min on foot. Bus from Lagos to Salema (Timetable 2), then use the map to walk to Boca do Rio.
A stony but secluded beach, with the added interest of Roman remains and ancient salt pans. No shade.

4a PRAIA DO ZAVIAL (map pages 66-67) ○

🚗 by car or taxi: no walking. Park at the back of the beach. Heading west on the N125 towards Sagres, turn left at the Raposeira traffic lights to Hortas do Tabual. Zavial is 4km from Raposeira; keep ahead as the road forks right to Ingrina. The road continues past Zavial to Ingrina, then turns back to Raposeira.
A deep stretch of sandy beach with a further beach beyond the rocks to the left. Popular with surfers, but be aware of strong currents. Café/ restaurant on the beach, mainly open on weekends/holidays in winter. Usually, if Zavial's café is closed, Ingrina's will open — and vice-versa.

4b PRAIA DA INGRINA (map pages 66-67) ○

🚗 by car or taxi: no walking. Park just off the road behind the beach or at the side of the café. Follow the instructions for Picnic 4a to the fork after Raposeira and turn right to Ingrina, reached 4.5km/2.8mi from Raposeira.
A smaller, more open stretch of sandy beach than Zavial, and with easier access to coastal walks. The café is immediately behind the beach and is often open in winter, especially at weekends (see under Zavial above).

9 SILVES WINDMILL (map pages 84-85; photograph page 82) ○

🚗 by car or taxi: 32min on foot. Park in the large car park by the river below the town and follow the notes for Walk 9.
🚌 🚆 by bus or train: 32min on foot. Bus or train from Portimão to Silves (Timetables 4, 9), then follow the notes for Walk 9.
A wonderful panoramic location, carpeted with flowers in springtime.

10a PRAIA DA MARINHA (map page 86) ○

🚗 only accessible by car or taxi: 4min on foot. To reach Marinha, turn south off the N125 opposite the International School, heading towards Benagil. (This school is located 3km east of the Lagoa roundabout and 2km west of Porches.) Some 4km down this road, turn left at the road signposted 'Praia da Marinha'. Park in car park on the cliff top above the beach and follow Walk 10 from the 26min-point.
Breathtaking — a magnificent beach! Very natural, with limited facilities and little shade. Café/bar in season.

10b PRAIA DE ALBANDEIRA (map page 86) ○

🚗 only accessible by car or taxi: up to 22min on foot. To reach Praia

View from the mill at Barreiras Brancas (Picnic CT3b)

de Albandeira, turn south towards Benagil opposite the International School (see 10a above). After 3km, turn left along the narrow road signposted 'Praia de Albandeira'. Park behind the beach (no walking). Alternatively, park as for Picnic 10a and follow Walk 10 from the 26min-point (22min).
An out-of-the-way spot with facilities in season; no shade.

12 FONTE GRANDE, ALTE (map pages 96-97; nearby photograph pages 94-95)

🚗 only accessible by car or taxi: no walking. Park at the picnic site, by following the notes for Car tour 3 on page 31.
An official picnic site by the river where trees provide ample shade. Full facilities available in season and on holidays; public WC.

13 PADERNE CASTLE (map page 101; photograph page 99)

🚗 by car or taxi: no walking, or up to 29min on foot. Either drive direct to the castle, or park on the main road near the road signposted 'Fonte' and follow Walk 13 from the 3min-point.
🚌 by bus: 32min on foot. Bus from Albufeira to Paderne (Timetable 7), then follow the notes for Walk 13.
Lovely viewpoint from an old Moorish castle set in the heart of the countryside.

15 ROCHA DA PENA (map pages 108-109; photograph page 105)

🚗 only accessible by car or taxi: 7min on foot. Park as for Walk 15 and follow the walking notes as far as the 7min-point.
Picnic under the carob trees and enjoy extensive views out over the farmland below. Café/bar at Fonte Amoados.

16 SALIR (map pages 108-109; photograph page 111)

🚗 only accessible by car or taxi: 5min on foot. Park on the wide road below the village, as in Car tour 3, then head up towards the church and water tower. Refer to Walk 16, from the 2h-point, to visit the castle.
Extensive, superb panorama from this strategic viewpoint.

18 RUINED WATER-MILL (map page 117) ○

🚗 by car or taxi: 12min on foot. From São Brás follow signs to

Almargens, then Tareja. Tareja is on the left, further along the road past the entrance to the rehabilitation centre. Park near the track off left just past Tareja, before the surfaced road ends (there is a fountain below left). Walk down the track to the left (with a stream below on your right). Within 10min keep ahead, as a track goes off right. You reach the river and ruined watermill 2min later.

🚌 by bus: 52min on foot. Bus from Faro to São Brás (Timetable 6). Follow the notes for Walk 18 as far as the 36min-point, where you turn right along the surfaced road to reach a track and fountain on the left in 40min. Turn left down the track and follow the notes for motorists above.

A tranquil and secluded riverside setting by a ruined watermill. If you have children with you, keep them out of the watermill which has a small but uncovered deep hole inside, possibly a well.

CT1 BARRAGEM DA BRAVURA (see the touring map) ○

🚗 only accessible by car or taxi: no walking. Park in the car park by the restaurant at the dam *(barragem)*, reached by following the notes for Car tour 1 as far as the 24km-point at Odiáxere (page 18) and turning right in the centre. The narrow surfaced road leads in 9km to the dam. Just before descending to the car park, there is another car parking area on the left, which is a good viewpoint. This is also a marvellous area in spring for a variety of wild flowers.

Situated amongst the rolling matos-covered hills with a view of the Serra de Monchique.

CT2a BARRAGEM DO ARADE (see the touring map) ○

🚗 only accessible by car or taxi: no walking. Park in the car park to the left as you arrive at the dam *(barragem)*. The surfaced road to the dam is on the right, 10km from São Bartolomeu de Messines in the direction of Silves, or on the left 7km from Silves (Car tour 2, page 23). It is then a further 3.5km down this road to the *barragem*.

On the edge of the matos-covered hills so typical of inland Algarve, this dam has the added interest of an island which can be visited by boat. Facilities include a restaurant/café, sunbathing terrace, boat hire.

CT2b CALDAS DE MONCHIQUE (see the touring map)

🚗 by car or taxi: no walking. Park in the car park in Caldas (see Car tour 2, page 24).

🚌 by bus: little walking. Bus from Portimão to Caldas de Monchique (Timetable 3); alight at the road leading down into Caldas.

Pleasant shaded areas where you can enjoy the ambience of this ancient spa.

CT3a FONTE DE BENÉMOLA (see the touring map) ○

🚗 only accessible by car or taxi: 20min on foot. See Circular walk for motorists on pages 28-29 for details on how to get there and park.

A river location hidden in the depths of pastoral countryside.

CT3b BARREIRAS BRANCAS (see the touring map; photograph opposite) ○

🚗 only accessible by car or taxi: 20min on foot. See Circular walk for motorists, page 30, for details on how to get there and park.

Share this lovely vantage point with an old windmill.

❀ Touring

Algarve is a fascinating region to explore, offering a varied choice of landscapes. Sometimes, relatively short distances can take a long time to cover, due to the winding nature of the road. But travel across much of Algarve has improved considerably in recent years, due to good new roads and a motorway, the Via do Infante (A22).

Although there is a good bus and train service for the coastal regions, it is difficult to reach inland areas easily. Hiring a car gives you the freedom to see and savour the varied countryside at your own pace, as well as allowing forays off the beaten track. The countryside road network in Algarve is very variable — from very good to virtually impassable, all probably taking longer to drive than you may perhaps anticipate.

There is a fairly wide selection of **touring maps**. But old editions are often mixed in with the new, *so check the date before buying*. New motorways, and road systems generally, have made getting around much easier and may provide optional routes for the car tours. The map in the book shows major routes and some minor routes, all of which are as accurate as they can be.

Car hire is inexpensive out of the main season (April to October). It is preferable to stay with the well-known hire companies, through whom you can arrange and pay for your car hire before you leave. This arrangement usually includes all taxes, including CDW, and unlimited mileage. There are also very reasonable fly-drive offers, especially outside the main tourist season.

Take care when renting; check the car and take time to study the **rental conditions/insurance coverage**. It is imperative to ensure that 'collision damage waiver' is included in the insurance, to cover damage to your hire car if repair costs cannot be recovered from a third party. Tyre and windscreen damage (including punctures) are the responsibility of the hirer, so check carefully before you drive off, including the spare. Always carry the agency's phone number with you, and take some water, food, and warm clothing in case of breakdown.

The wearing of **seat belts** is compulsory, and locals comply outside the main towns, but there seems to be some unspoken agreement that they aren't necessary in built-up areas. Always wear your seat belt! Rear seat belts must also be worn, and children under 13 are not allowed as front seat passengers.

Petrol stations are frequent along the N125, and many of them are open seven days a week; some of the international companies offer a 24-hour service. There are fewer petrol stations in country areas, and many are closed on Sunday. If you are heading inland, go with a full tank of petrol. Some grades of petrol may be unfamiliar: *super* is self-explanatory, as is *diesel,* but *sem chumbo* = unleaded. A petrol station by the roundabout at the entrance to Faro airport is convenient for those returning hire cars.

Drive carefully: the road is regarded as a walkway, especially in country areas. Be extra vigilant for animals and the large-wheeled carts still encountered in the country. Be aware also that even main roads almost invariably narrow appreciably where they cross bridges and sometimes where they pass through small villages; there are usually no warnings.

There has been a vast improvement in the **standard of driving**, but be wary — particularly with regard to overtaking. The N125 along the coast is still treated as a motorway by some locals. It is mainly a single-lane flow, with an additional lane at the side for breakdowns and very slow moving traffic like farm tractors. In some places there are short, well signposted stretches, expressly for overtaking.

The significance of **zebra crossings** is confusing, as there are no beacons to indicate their presence, but they are generally respected. Many traffic lights and junctions have been replaced by **roundabouts** *(rotundas)* — a recent discovery here in Algarve. **Road markings** have also been greatly improved in recent years.

There are frequent **police checks**, so it is essential for the driver to have the relevant documents relating to the vehicle, driving licence and passport to hand if a heavy fine is to be avoided.

Remember to take a **pocket phrase-book**, if only for the road signs; you won't find them written in English. A parking sign depicting what looks like a comb and a car = park at an angle to the road to maximise parking space; *perigo* = danger; *desvio* = diversion; *lombas* = a ridge in the road to slow traffic. (The intriguing 'Património do Estado' engraved on many buildings and monuments simply translates to 'government property'.)

Telephones are widely available, but only take phone cards; otherwise hotels, restaurants, bars and shops will let you use their phones (but check the unit rates first). **Mobiles** need a roaming agreement for use abroad. **WCs** are available in most towns — in market halls, supermarkets, bus and railway stations, restaurants, cafes and some petrol stations. Don't always rely on toilet paper being supplied; carry your own.

The **touring notes** are brief: they include little history or information about the towns. Some literature is available from tourist offices, and sometimes we refer you to the walking notes for more comment but, for more information, see our background reading list on page 6. We concentrate mainly on the 'logistics' of touring: times and distances, road conditions, viewpoints and good places to rest. Most of all we emphasise possibilities for **walking** and **picnicking**; for information about the picnic spots highlighted in the notes, see pages 8-13. If you want to stretch your legs, look at the short walks listed with the main walks. This should give you a taste of the landscapes, sufficient to whet your appetite for more.

There are many centres of tourism along the coast of Algarve, all of which can easily be keyed into the routes of the car tours from our chosen starting points. Three of the tours start in the east, from Faro, and two in the west, from the Lagoa roundabout on the N125.

Allow plenty of time for **stops**: our times include only short breaks at viewpoints labelled (☎) in the touring notes. Distances quoted are *cumulative km* from Faro or the Lagoa roundabout. A key to the symbols in the notes is on the touring map.

If you only hire a car for one day, Tour 1, a long trip, provides a sampler, encompassing the windswept coast and the pastoral serenity of the Serra de Monchique. If you don't wish to drive quite as far, Tour 3 takes you through an appealing and gentler countryside, punctuated by the intriguing *rochas* of Pena and Soidos. Most of our hire cars recorded whole kilometres only, so our distances are not always accurate to the nearest decimal place, which left us guessing a little at some distances below a kilometre. This shouldn't cause any problems when used in conjunction with the other instructions.

All motorists should read the country code on pages 48-49 and go quietly in the countryside.

Country fairs and markets

Market day is a day of great atmosphere and excitement for the local people. It is a chance to look for bargains, shop for locally-grown produce, buy goods that are not normally available in the local shops, or even sell or buy some livestock. Just about everything is on offer at some of the larger markets, and it is particularly those with a livestock section that are best described as 'country fairs'. Here temporary bars and eating places are set up, where the menfolk seal most of their bargains.

None of this is window-dressing for tourism, so here is an opportunity to see at first hand the ordinary life of the local people, to observe and appreciate their customs. It is a snapshot on life. You might also be tempted to buy; some of the home-produced honey is good value, as is bedding and towelling. If you feel like a snack while you are walking around, try the *farturas,* which look like doughnut rings — but make sure they are hot.

The markets are held on a regular timetable, most of them taking place monthly.

Weekly markets

Saturdays: Loulé, São Brás   Wednesdays: Quarteira

Fortnightly market

Tuesdays (1st and 3rd in the month): Albufeira

Monthly markets

1st Sunday: Moncarapacho	1st Monday: Portimão
1st Friday: Sagres	1st Saturday: Lagos
2nd Sunday: Estói*	2nd Monday: Algoz*
3rd Monday: Silves	3rd Thursday: Alte
4th Saturday: Tunes	4th Monday: Messines

*These are two of the bigger markets — really country fairs

Grilling sardines at an outdoor restaurant in Portimão

1 THE WEST COAST TOUR

Lagoa • Portimão • Lagos • Sagres • Aljezur • Marmelete • Silves • Lagoa

196km/122mi; about 4 hours' driving: start from the Lagoa roundabout, on the N125, heading west towards Portimão.

On route: Picnics (see pages 8-13) 1, 3a-c, 4a-b, 9, (10a, 10b), CT1, CT2a-b; Walks 1-9, (10)

On the whole, all the roads are well surfaced.

Visit the pleasant resort of Lagos and enjoy a spectacular coastline which still harbours a few relatively-unspoilt fishing villages. Windswept Sagres, one time home of Prince Henry the Navigator, is now a favoured spot for fishermen who hang precariously from the rocky cliffs at dizzy heights, casting their lines into the waves below. Follow the Atlantic coastline northwards, past deserted sandy beaches. Visit the castle at Aljezur, before turning inland to yet more dramatic scenery, as you head towards the highest mountain range in Algarve.

Starting from the roundabout at **Lagoa** on the N125, head west towards Portimão. Almost immediately there is a left turn to a 'water slide' park, but keep ahead on the N125 (or use the A22 to go directly to Lagos). Take the next right turn to Portimão in 5km. The road leads back under the N125 and into town over the old narrow bridge. Turn left immediately on crossing the bridge and head for the centre of **Portimão** (10km 🏨🛏️✕🚏⊕🛒WC). To park, keep heading south in the one-way system and, once beyond the centre, follow signs left to Faro. This leads you back along the river, where you can park. (To continue directly to Lagos from here, head back to the old bridge. Don't cross the bridge; turn left and follow signs to Lagos, to rejoin the N125.)

Leave Portimão by heading south, parallel with the river, to **Praia da Rocha** (13km 🏨🛏️✕🛒). A left turn on reaching the promenade leads to the remains of the 16th-century fort of Santa Catarina which guarded the mouth of the River Arade, once navigable to Silves. Now the fort provides a good viewpoint across the river to Ferragudo and the 17th-century fort of São João.

From Praia da Rocha follow the coast road west to **Vau** and on to the old fishing village of **Alvor** (18km). The road now swings inland, to meet the N125 in a further 4km (21.5km), at the end of the Portimão bypass. Turn left, where our route continues ahead through pleasant countryside. At **Odiáxere** (24km) the road narrows to pass between the houses. In the centre of the village, you could turn right to the Barragem da Bravura (📷✕*P*CT1a).

The shimmering white town of Lagos and the bridge over the Ribeira de Bensafrim are swiftly reached. Once across the bridge, turn left at the roundabout then negotiate further roundabouts to head into **Lagos★** (29km Π✝▲▲▲✕⛽Δ▮**M**WC). Continue alongside the river for just over 1km from the third roundabout, where you will find car parks and plenty of parking on the roadside.

To continue the tour, stay with the riverside road, which sweeps up past the fort and round the back of Lagos; follow signs to Sagres. (Ponta da Piedade, Porto de Mós and Praia Dona Ana — all visited on Walk 1; photographs pages 6 and 56 — are signposted off left.) Keep ahead at the roundabout, where a right turn heads back to Faro. The pretty, gently undulating countryside along this next stretch of road is very appealing. Pass the turn-off to Luz (✝▲▲▲✕Δ▮WC***P***1; Walks 1 and 2) in 40km; the village is 3km down the road to the left. Once past **Espiche**, after 48km, notice the left turn to Burgau★ (▲✕▮WC; Walk 3). Burgau, shown on pages 21 and 53, is 2km down the road, and Ponta da Almádena (***P***3a, 3b) a further 2km west from there. *Matos*-covered rolling hills with pockets of cultivation lie beyond the tree-lined road. This soon takes on a wilder aspect once you pass **Vale de Boi** (51km). Soon after **Budens** (51.5km Π) watch for a left turn (52.5km) signposted to Salema. This turn-off leads to both Figueira (Walk 4) and Salema★ (▲▲▲✕▮WC***P***3c; Walk 3).

There are fewer signs of habitation here, as the *matos,* now becoming stunted in growth due to the windswept location, invades the countryside. After passing the Salema turn-off, turn right onto the old road, signposted to Guadalupe. This leads to the chapel of Nossa Senhora de Guadalupe, where Henry the Navigator is once thought to have worshipped. Continue along the old road which soon rejoins the N125. At **Raposeira** (59km) a left turn at the traffic lights gives access to the beaches of Zavial and Ingrina (Δ***P***4a-b). Around here large tracts of pastureland dominate the scenery. This gives way to green and well-farmed, gently-rolling hills as you approach **Vila do Bispo** (61km ✝✕), where you keep round left towards Sagres on the main road (N268). An obvious absence of trees, except for those lining the road, announces the windswept and wild nature of this narrow strip of land jutting out into the Atlantic.

As you approach a roundabout (70km), the frontage of a fort fills in the landscape. Keep ahead to visit the **Forta-**

leza de Sagres (71km): park in the large car park outside. Inside, there is a huge pebble wind-compass *(rosa dos ventos)*, a chapel (photograph page 25), a café and an indifferent museum. You can also walk out to Sagres lighthouse at the end of the promontory (📷) and watch the local men fishing from precarious perches over-hanging the sea far below. Return to the roundabout and turn right into **Sagres★** (**🏔🏚✕🏤🍺**). Almost imme-diately there is a square on the right which is a pleasant café area, from where it is about 1km further down to the fishing harbour.

Head back to the roundabout to continue towards Cape St Vincent; the road heads straight through low scrub towards the lighthouse at the cape. Although the elements may have tried to subdue growth in this corner of Algarve, the botanist may well be surprised at the variety of flora awaiting discovery amongst the cowering bushes. Just before reaching the lighthouse, there is another fort on the right, the Fortaleza de Beliche (79km ✕). **Cabo de São Vicente** (Cape St Vincent) is reached in 80km. The position of the lighthouse, 9° west of Greenwich, makes it one of the most westerly points in Europe. Unfortunately the lighthouse grounds are closed to the public. From this viewpoint the Sagres lighthouse and the white-walled bulk of the fort can be clearly seen. One word of caution. If a gale is blowing in the rest of Algarve, save your visit for another day, as this area is windswept at the best of times.

Retrace your route back to **Vila do Bispo** (96km) and turn right to loop over the road (signposted for Aljezur and Lisbon). The tree-lined N268 now runs parallel with the coast through softer, more undulating terrain. From **Carrapateira** (110km 🍺), an isolated spot, roads lead off left to mainly-deserted sandy beaches. Pockets of green cultivation make patterns among the *matos*-covered low hills. There's a new, signposted walk (15km) leaving from a large lay-by on the left as you approach **Bordeira** (114km). You may like to try the short version, or do the whole walk another day; see STOP PRESS on page 136.

When you meet the main Lagos/Lisbon road (N120; 124km), turn left on the N120. As you approach Aljezur you will see the castle on the hill above the town. Drive through **Aljezur** (130km 🛈🏚🏔✕🏤📷🍺WC), where the main road sweeps round right and over a bridge. Park on the left, just over the bridge, by the tourist office. To walk up to the castle (ten minutes), cross back over the river on a footbridge, to a small square. With your back towards the river, take the cobbled road up from the far right-hand corner of the square and continue round to the left, to climb through old Aljezur. When you meet a track, turn left up to the castle. Nothing much remains of it besides the walls, which look impressive from below, a vaulted cistern and two towers. The castle provides an excellent viewpoint, however: looking inland, Fóia, the highest peak in Algarve and the setting for Walk 6, can be spotted in the distance.

Leave the car park and turn left towards Lisbon; almost immediately there is a junction, where you go right (N267) towards Marmelete and Monchique. This is a spectacular run along a high-level road (🕾) which wends ever upwards, crossing a narrow ridge where valleys plunge down steeply on either side. Pretty hollows of cultivation and rolling *matos*-covered hills — which become a carpet of white flowers in spring — catch the eye (🕾). The road surface is good.

As you start to descend (142.5km) there are glimpses of the Barragem da Bravura not too far to the right (🕾). Fóia, the highest point, distinguished by its attendant cluster of antennae, can also be seen ahead. Beyond **Marmelete** (146km ♥🎒), woodland softens and cloaks the landscape, as the left turn to Chilrão (152km; Walk 5) is soon passed. On the approach to **Casais** (155km) the trees screening the roadside part to reveal views to the right over the countryside.

ROGIL NATURE RESERVE — *Short walk for motorists*

This is an easy and delightful short walk (2.5km/1.6mi; 1h) through sand dunes, which are home to a variety of coastal flora. Tread carefully!
From Aljezur, drive to the far end of Rogil and turn left to Esteveira. Park in the open area on the right on meeting cross tracks in 3.2km, where the road ends. Start from the car park by keeping left, seawards, along the track — to head between two red-roofed white houses. As the track becomes sandy (4min), fork left onto a path.
There are a few sandy paths but, basically, just walk south along the cliff top. In around 30min, the path swings inland, with a gully over to the right and pine trees on the left. Continue circling left, edging the pine wood, until the car park comes into view ahead. Do not walk across the fields, but stay on the path which heads right, back to the track, just before the houses met on the way out. Turn right on meeting the track back to the car park.

Landscape on the Penina/Casais road

Suddenly, as you penetrate further into the **Serra de Monchique**, the scene changes yet again, as deep terraced valleys create an interesting alpine picture (📷; photographs pages 77 and 91).

Turn right downhill towards Portimão on reaching the main road at **Nave** (N266; 159km).* In 3km pass the 'Miradouro das Caldas' (✗🅰📷) on the right, which is a good viewpoint over Caldas de Monchique. Continue to wind downhill on a good surfaced road and, if you have time to visit Caldas★ (🛏🛈✗🅿🅰♨WC *P*CT2b; Car tour 2), turn right in a little over 1km. This right turn, the only vehicular access into the centre of Caldas, is difficult from this approach, as it is an acutely-angled turn back the way you came. Soon reach a roundabout (163km), the exit from the one-way system through Caldas; this is also an access point for the spa hotel and the water bottling plant, so it is possible to turn right here and park at the end of the one-way system, leaving a five-minute walk to the centre.

Once down from the hills (169.5km), the wooded areas are left behind, and the road straightens out as it heads towards Portimão. At the **Porto de Lagos** roundabout (175.5km), turn left for Silves on the N124. (Or, for a quicker return to Lagoa, keep ahead to join the A22 on the outskirts of Portimão and turn left towards Faro.) Enjoy some tranquil scenery as you drive along this well-surfaced road, passing Walk 8 en route, to **Silves★** (186.5km ▮🕆🛏✗ 🅿⊕🅰M♨wc*P*9; Walk 9; Car tour 2). If you wish to stop in Silves, which is up on the left, park in the car park on the right or alongside the road skirting the town. See Walk 9 for more details, and photograph page 82.

Continue back to Lagoa by turning right over the river below Silves (188km), and then turn right again. This leads you back onto the N125, where you can turn left, back to the **Lagoa roundabout** (196km).

*A left turn would take you up to Monchique★ (🕆🛏✗🅿⊕♨WC; Walks 5, 6, 7). See Car tour 2 for more details about Monchique.

2 MOUNTAINS AND 'MOORS'

Lagoa • Silves • Caldas de Monchique • Monchique • Fóia • Lagoa

91km/57mi; about 2 hours' driving: start from Lagoa roundabout, on the main N125, and head north to Silves.

On route: Picnics (see pages 8-13) 9, CT2a, 2b; Walks 5-9

The road up from Monchique to Fóia is narrow, but wide enough for two cars. If possible, save this tour for a day when you can see the Serra de Monchique clearly from Lagoa, so that you will be able fully to appreciate the superb views.

Highlights on this memorable tour include the imposing remains at Silves — the Moors' capital of Algarve, an ancient spa set amidst soft green foliage and recalling days gone by, and the breathtaking views from the highest point in the tour, Fóia.

From **Lagoa** (🕇🛆✕🚗🍴) head west on the N125. At the A22 access roundabout, turn inland towards the motorway (Junction 6) and follow signs to Silves. There are good views of the castle on the descent towards Silves (📷). At **Silves★** (🏠🕇🛆✕🚗⊕🎋🍴MWC*P*9; Walk 9; photograph page 82). The castle ramparts glow red in early morning or evening sunlight. Turn left over the river and left again at the T-junction (7.5km).* There is a large car park and also parking along the roadside on the right. See the notes with Walk 9 (page 82) for more information about Silves and to guide you up to the town centre. Besides the interesting historical remains and a museum, the daily market in Silves, almost opposite the old bridge, is excellent for fresh produce.

Leave Silves and continue west in the direction of Monchique. Some 4km from Silves roundabout, you pass the Mira-Rio restaurant on the left, where Walk 8 begins. A winding road now leads through pretty pastoral countryside, where oranges and lemons grow in abundance. This is a major orange-growing area, and en route to Monchique you will pass many roadside stalls selling oranges.

Meet a roundabout after 18.5km and turn right on the N266 towards Monchique and the mountains. A mass of purple from the many Judas trees lining the road here brings a splash of colour in spring. Enjoy a pleasant drive towards the foothills of the distinctive Serra de Monchique, past cultivated fields and through scattered

---

*A right turn at this T-junction leads in the direction of São Bartolomeu de Messines and the Barragem do Arade (✕*P*CT2a). This road passes the 'Cruz de Portugal', a 16th-century cross which is set on the left just past the next exit from Silves.

Once the capital of Algarve, Silves is now an orange-growing centre and pleasant place to take a break while touring (Car tours 1 and 2) or enjoying Walk 9.

hamlets. Fields give way to woodland as the road starts to wind and twist uphill (24.5km). This is a beautiful climb on days when the sun filtering through the trees casts dancing, shimmering shadows. Pass a very large shady lay-by on the right (28km), before reaching the roundabout exit from Caldas de Monchique on the left (29km). This is the entrance to the spa hotel and the water bottling plant, but the exit for the one-way system through Caldas itself. It is possible to turn left here and park near the end of the one-way system, leaving a five-minute walk into Caldas centre. To visit **Caldas de Monchique★** (🏔🛏⛪✖🕭🚌WC *P*CT2b) by car, fork left at the next road (29.5km) and park by the roadside or in the centre car park (30km). Caldas has just undergone a major renovation, intended to restore the village to the spa centre it once was.

Leave Caldas by the one-way system and turn left to continue to wind up in the direction of Monchique, again passing the fork down left to Caldas (31km) a few moments later. A further 1.3km brings you to a superb viewpoint over Caldas on the left, the **Miradouro das Caldas** (✖🕭🌄).

At **Nave** (34.5km) there is a left turn to Marmelete opposite a quarry on the right, but keep ahead for Monchique. Just after a petrol station on the left, as you enter Monchique, come to a crossroads (36.5km).* Keep straight on up to the Largo 5 de Outubro in **Monchique★** (🚻🛏✖🚌⊕🚾WC; Walks 5-7), where you can park in the square on the left, in a lay-by to the right, or up the Fóia

*A right turn here would take you to Alferce (🕭; 16km return) or 28.4km down to meet the N266 above Porto de Lagos; see touring map). There are wonderful views along this route.

Car tour 1: one of a series of tiled friezes in Lagos, depicting the Stations of the Cross (above), and chapel in the Fortaleza de Sagres

road on the left. It is worthwhile trying the first part of Walk 5 as far as the convent. This guides you up through old Monchique to a good vantage point from where it's possible to enjoy views (🎦) across the valley in the direction of Picota (Walk 7).

Continue through the square and up left towards Fóia (38km). Go right at the small roundabout soon encountered. The road now rises rapidly above Monchique. Fantastic views open out to the left (🎦) as you climb through eucalyptus. When you reach the point where the vegetation starts to become more sparse (44km), there is a *fonte* and *miradouro* on the left; Walk 5 begins on the next track off left, reached almost immediately.

The final 2km drive up to the summit, through mainly low-lying heather and cistus, provides almost uninterrupted views (🎦) over the countryside to the left. On the approach to **Fóia** (✗🎦▮), keep left to the car park. The summit is unfortunately home to a forest of television and radio masts, as well as a souvenir complex. But if you follow the notes for Short walk 6-2 (page 74) for about ten minutes, these will take you off the summit and to the fine views shown on pages 74-75.

Return to the main N266 (54km) by going right at the roundabout, then turn right in the direction of Portimão, following your outward route back to **Lagoa** (91km)*.

*An optional return is via Alferce (see footnote opposite), down to Odelouca (on the N124) and back via Silves to Lagoa.

3 VILLAGES OF THE BARROCAL

Faro • Estói • Amendoeira • (Fonte de Benémola) • Salir • Alte • Paderne • Boliqueime • Faro

105km/65mi; about 2 hours 20 minutes' driving: leave Faro from the harbour (see town plan on the reverse of the touring map).

On route: Picnics (see pages 8-13) 12, 13, 15, 16, CT3a, 3b; Walks 11-13, 15-17. (Walk 14 is nearby.)

On the whole, the country roads used on this tour are well surfaced. Petrol is usually available inland, but make sure you have enough before setting out, especially on Sundays and holidays.

Opening hours
Estói, Palace gardens: open 09.00-12.30, 14.00-17.30; closed Sundays, Mondays and holidays
Milreu: open 09.30-12.30, 14.00-18.00; closed Mondays and holidays

A pink palace, some Roman ruins, a Moorish castle, gently-rolling pastoral countryside, and sleepy inland villages weave a fascinating tapestry into the central limestone region of Algarve — the Barrocal, described on pages 90 and 91.

The tour starts from **Faro**. If a visit to old Faro is part of your tour, the best place to park is in Largo de São Francisco; otherwise, avoid the centre of Faro with its confusing one-way system. A proliferaton of new road systems around Faro should make navigation quite easy. Start the tour by joining the N2 to São Brás, which also gives access to the A22 at Junction 14.

The N2 leads you quickly out across the plain to the Algarvian foothills and to the right turn to São Brás and Estói. Fork off right to Estói after 10km and turn right at the crossroads shortly afterwards. At the ruins of **Milreu** (10.2km 🚻), park outside on the left. (See Walk 17, page 112, for more details about this interesting site with many excavated remains to be seen.) On leaving Milreu continue into **Estói**★ (11km ◗◖WC). As you enter the main square, you can see the gates of the palace up to your left. Turn right and park further along this road. The gates give access to the gardens, where the photograph opposite was taken. They are worth a visit for their curiosity value, but the palace itself (eventually to be converted into a government *pousada*) is not open to the public. If you would like a closer look at the palace buildings, go up steps at the right of the gates, then turn left and left again.

Return by the same route back to the main road to São Brás, and turn right immediately after crossing the bridge at the minor crossroads. You pass a petrol station on the left, just before meeting the main N2, where you turn

26

right. Just 100m further on (after passing under the A22), take the left turn signposted to Bordeira (12.5km). A scenic route along winding country roads, through lovely rural countryside like that shown on pages 114-115, raises you gently into the rolling hills (📷). Just after a sharp bend to the left, meet significant-looking crossroads (19km) and keep ahead to the main Loulé/São Brás road (N270; 20km). Turn left, and be ready to turn right almost immediately (signposted 'São Romão' and 'Alportel'),

Narrow street in old Albufeira

FONTE DE BENÉMOLA — *Circular walk for motorists*

Buried deep in the countryside is a little known beauty spot by a river, the Fonte de Benémola. It is just a short waymarked walk of about 3.5km/ 2.2mi, taking around 40min, to this beauty spot and back — or 50min, if you complete the whole circuit. If you are in the area, or if you want a break during Car tour 3, then try it as a short walk or for a picnic outing.

Follow the notes for Car tour 3 to the 32km-point, on the N524, where you keep ahead towards Tor, instead of turning right. Look for a track on the right about 1km further on, signposted 'Fonte de Benémola'. Park off the road, by the abandoned house on the left, as you enter the track — or at a convenient place on the road.

Start walking down the track along the side of a shallow valley (the locals drive here, but we would like to discourage you from doing so). The deep green foliage of the orange trees and the ordered cultivation down on the left contrasts sharply with the scrubland up to the right. It is this scrubland, however, which shelters a wealth of wild flowers, including *Astragalus lusitanicus*, with its creamy-yellow pea-like flowers, the cheerful yellow *Anemone*

---

back onto a country road. Rise up through **São Romão** and come to a fork (21km), where you go left towards Amendoeira. Striking deeper into the hinterland, the rural aspect gives way to a more barren landscape. *Matos,* interspersed with pockets of cultivation, becomes more predominant as you near **Amendoeira** (24km). Reach the main Loulé/Barranco do Velho road and turn right (N396; 27km). Stay on this road for a short while, through **Porto Nobre** (28km), where pine trees lining the road give a more alpine feel to the surroundings. Fork off left towards 'Querença' and 'Tor' after 30km, and ignore a left turn to Querença shortly afterwards.

Keep along the road towards Tor, until you turn right towards 'Alte' and 'Lisbon' in 32km. (Keep ahead here for a further 1km, if you wish to visit the Fonte de Benémola, setting for *P*CT3a; see circular walk suggestion above.) Here is yet another twisting road which wends its way through undulating countryside, past almond groves and through hamlets (🎦). Watch out for some sharp bends along this stretch. The route of Walk 16 joins in from the left after 37km and stays with the road for 400m before departing off left on a field track. On arriving at the main N124, the São Bartolomeu de Messines/Barranco do Velho road (38km), turn left.

First head for Salir and pass the point where Walk 16 again meets the main road from the left (38.5km) and continues on the track opposite. The white water tower of Salir is easily distinguishable ahead, as you drive along *palmata*, and a number of orchids. At a fork (**10min**), keep left. Head down towards a stream and the leafy shade of a natural beauty spot, where you cross a bridge over the stream. Turn left when the track divides beyond the bridge (**12min**). Orange, lemon and carob trees cluster together on the left, the scent of the citrus flowers providing an added delight in spring. Keep left at the next division, in just under **14min**, staying ahead, with the river on your left, to reach the *fonte* in **20min** and then the picnic area beyond it (*P*CT3a). It is possible to explore further upstream, where the river flows through a small ravine and where there are some caves close by to the right.

To continue, cross the river on the good stepping stones *opposite the picnic area* and go left again on the track, downstream. Keep the river on your left and stay on the main track. A basket-maker can usually be found sitting outside his hut just below the return track, where baskets of varying sizes can be bought at reasonable prices. When you emerge by a bridge on the N524, turn left to cross the bridge, and follow the road round to the left, back to where you parked (five minutes away).

Or return to where you parked by the same outward route.

---

past a scattering of white traditional houses. Take the left-hand turn up to **Salir** (✝✕🖼🍴*P*16) at 42km; note that it is signposted to Loulé and comes up when you have almost passed the village. This road leads uphill and skirts round the village, which is on the left. Follow the road and keep right towards Loulé. Park on the roadside below the village, about 0.9km from the main road. Head left up into the village on foot to explore the centre (photograph page 111) and perhaps take in the setting for Picnic 16. If you are doing Walk 16, park further along the wide road, about 1.3km from the main road (where the road bends right down to 'Ponte de Salir' and 'Loulé'). For more details about Salir, see the notes for Walk 16 on page 108.

Return to the main N124 by the same route to continue, and turn left. As you drive along (🖼), you can't fail to notice the huge ridge of Rocha da Pena (Walk 15) to the right. About 1km beyond Salir, at **Taipa**, note the access road on the right to Rocha, where Walk 15 begins at a *fonte* (*P*15). Then come into **Pena**, where there is a local craft and information centre located in the old school (the last building on the right at the far end of the village). **Benafim** is soon reached (51km 🍴), and here the road narrows to pass between the houses. At 56km, note the narrow road off left — just before a sharp right-hand bend in the road, which can catch you unawares: it is our return route on this tour.

Some 200m further along, on entering the confines of

BARREIRAS BRANCAS —
Circular walk for motorists

This is a very short walk of 4km/2.5mi, taking about 50min, for those driving around the Loulé area. To get there, turn north at the central roundabout in Loulé (note the kilometre reading), to pass the bus station on the left. Then, at the crossroads before the monument, turn right, following the 'Querença' sign. This sets you on the Barranco do Velho road. Once beyond an avenue of cypress trees, look for a parking spot just before the start of a similar avenue (3km out of Loulé). Park on the right, near a small engineering works and restaurant, opposite a café. A windmill on a hill is your destination.

Start the walk from the engineering works, by heading down the right-hand track between the workshop on the left and the restaurant on the right. The track leads between orange groves to a bridge over a stream which is crossed in 3min. Continue ahead, and ignore two tracks on the right as you start to ascend. Turn right into a track, waymarked with a yellow stripe (8min). Keep an eye out on the left for a narrower walled-in path within two minutes; it leads you up the hillside in a gentle ascent. This old route hides some interesting flowers like the broad leaved *Epipactis helleborine* and the bright yellow *Anemone palmata*. Stay right in 11min, when the walled-in path runs into track and, as you continue to rise, you can enjoy views of Loulé to the right and the sea beyond. Meet a surfaced road in 14min, turn left in the direction of the windmill and, less than a minute later, stay ahead to a rough track (where the road swings right). At the next fork go left, above the peach-coloured house. In 16min, when the track divides, turn right; stay alongside the rock wall on the left to its end, then follow the path off left up to the windmill (19min; *P*CT3b). Whilst nothing much remains to see of the mill workings, there is a splendid panorama to be enjoyed from this location (see page 12). It is a good site for orchids, too, including the man orchid, *Aceras anthropophorum*, and the sombre bee orchid, *Ophrys fusca*.

Leave from the door of the mill and follow the path which heads in the direction of Loulé. The path leads down and round to the right, to pass beneath the windmill, now up on the right. Keep ahead as the path runs into surfaced road. Follow the road downhill, briefly meeting the upward route, to a T-junction (11min below the mill). Turn right, still on surfaced road, and enjoy the rural surrounds. Cross a wide field track, to continue ahead along another track. Some five minutes later, note the second of two walled-in paths leaving from the right: this is the path you took up to the mill. Turn left soon, to follow the outward route back to the car.

Left to right: Aceras anthropophorum, Ophrys fusca, Anemone palmata

Alte, there is a road off right direct to Fonte Grande. The main tour goes first into Alte and then on to Fonte Grande but, if you wish to go there straight away, turn right here, follow the road round and cross the bridge. This brings you to the first large fountain and small picnic area on the right. A much larger picnic area and fountain (**P**12), with better facilities, is to the right, past and above the first fountain (photograph page 95, map page 97).

First explore Alte itself, by continuing another 0.7km along the main road, past the Fonte Grande turn-off. The road runs below the village, which rises up to the right, and crosses a bridge where there is an old mill and some waterfalls. Turn right at the roundabout; this leads directly into the centre of Alte and the start of Walk 12. In just 200m, pass the left turn up to Santa Margarida (📷 and Walk 11; photograph page 91) as you enter **Alte★** (♟♠✕⌂📷💵). Park where possible before the Santa Margarida turn-off or near the market stalls, where the road is wide. The village centre lies ahead, with its cafés and maze of narrow streets. It is possible to drive through the village to Fonte Grande, or you can walk there (follow the notes for Walk 12 on page 94 as far as the 12min-point).

When you are ready to leave Alte, return to the roundabout on the N124 and turn left. Retrace your route to the 56km point, just after a sharp left bend, and turn right into a narrow surfaced road (60km). This road wends its way across the shallow valley south of Alte, through low-lying vegetation, which allows for good views (📷) over the countryside. At the fork reached after 61.5km keep round to the right. Care is needed in the centre of the village of **Monte Brito**, where there is a right-angled bend and no view round the corner. As you drive along a straight stretch of road, it is easy to feel that you are on the major road but beware: in just over 65km a road joins from the right, and there is a 'Stop' sign for you to obey — with no road markings. The sign is often obscured by foliage. Keep ahead, then turn right about 1km further on. There is a further right and left turn as the route heads across country to Paderne in the distance.

As you reach **Paderne★** (69km ♟⊕💵), keep to the road which skirts round to the right. On meeting the main road in Paderne, turn right downhill to meet the Boli-queime road. Park near the stadium opposite this junction, to explore Paderne or stretch your legs with one of the versions of Walk 13 (**P**13; photograph page 99, map page 101). To drive to Paderne Castle, turn right past the cemetery on the left. A little further on there is a road off left to the 'Fonte' and Paderne Castle.

To return to Faro, turn left opposite the stadium towards Boliqueime, passing Paderne up to the left. (But those returning to Albufeira and environs should continue west to the main N270 at Purgatório, 0.5km further on, and turn left.) Reach **Boliqueime** and turn left onto the N125 (79km) in the direction of Faro. Alternatively, go left to Junction 11 on the A22, for a faster return to Faro. Leave at Junction 13 to return to **Faro** (**105km**).

Albufeira

4 EASTERN HIGHLIGHTS

Faro • Olhão • (Tavira) • Vila Real de Santo António • Castro Marim • Cachopo • Barranco do Velho • São Brás de Alportel • Faro

175km/109mi; about 3 hours 30 minutes' driving: leave Faro from the harbour (see town plan on the reverse of the touring map).

On route: Picnic (see pages 8-13) 18; Walks 16-20

Once off the N125, the inland roads become more winding and twisting. Make sure you have enough petrol before heading inland to Cachopo.

Vila Real is a bustling riverside town only a short ferry ride from Spain; nearby we find the tranquillity of a backwater, where the remains of a 14th-century castle stand sentinel to its past glory and importance. This tour penetrates deep into countryside still untouched by tourism, where you can relish an astoundingly beautiful landscape.

Start out from **Faro** along the N125 towards 'Espanha' (Spain), which will take you all the way to Vila Real and the Spanish border.

Olhão (✛▲▲♦✕△🏪⊕M⚎WC) is reached in 8km. Keep ahead on the main road at the first roundabout but, if you want to explore Olhão, turn right here to reach the centre. (A left turn at the same point would take you out to Estói, setting for Walk 17.) Pass a left turn to Moncarapacho and São Brás and then a right turn to Porto de Olhão (9km). Porto de Olhão is where you catch a ferry out to the barrier islands, where there are sandy beaches and shallow waters ideal for bathing — see page 37. Beyond Olhão the road surface becomes very good until you reach **Luz de Tavira** (22km), where you need to take care, as the road narrows. Note the Manueline doorway of the church on the left here. Continue along through flat cultivated countryside and scattered hamlets, where oranges, almonds and vines are important crops.

At the first roundabout, go right if you wish to visit Tavira★ (✛𝐈𝐓▲▲✕🏪⊕⚎WC)*. The main tour keeps ahead here, to reach the motorway roundabout (29km) and then a high-level road bridge. Note the left turn to Cachopo immediately after crossing the bridge; this is the road you will take on the return route. After the next roundabout (30km) the road off right is the exit from Tavira. Soon you are passing the large Eurotel complex on the left (32km), a landmark for those wishing to visit

*Park near the new market hall then continue over the new bridge to rejoin the N125 and continue the tour. Add about 3km to the overall distance for the tour, if you visit the town.

RAINY DAY SHOPPING OPTIONS

Algarve has moved rapidly into the world of big commercial centres.
Forum Algarve (Jumbo), on the airport side of Faro, and Algarve Shopping at Guia, near Albufeira, are both popular venues. These are reached from the N125 and house cinema complexes, restaurants and cafés, besides a huge supermarket and up-market shops.
Large supermarkets often have smaller retail shops and cafés within the same complex.

the Tavira National Forest for Walk 19. The left turn to the forest is 300m after the Eurotel and is signposted 'Mata de Conceição'.

After some 40km, the road narrows and curves to cross a bridge, then speedily carries you on in the direction of Vila Real. Just after the motorway slip road and a water sports centre on the left (46km), there is a left turn to 'Castro Marim' and 'Beja' (our return route). Keep ahead on the main road, to come into **Vila Real de Santo António**★ (♁▲▲▲⚒⛽⊕M▬WC), at 52km passing a roundabout with a left turn to Castro Marim. The road system in Vila Real is set out in a grid, so direction-finding is fairly straightforward. Follow the sign to the 'centro'; it directs you right, past the hospital on the left, and then left, down to the river. Entering on foot, you can follow the pedestrian walkway to the centre of town, by keeping ahead where the traffic is diverted to the right. Parking is allowed in some streets and along the riverside road. We find it easier to park on the outskirts and walk — especially if the town is busy. If you wish to visit Spain, a ferry still crosses the river regularly, taking about 15 minutes to cross, despite a road bridge further up the river.

Return to the Castro Marim roundabout (the 52km-point), and turn right on the N122. Gum and palm trees line the elevated road running straight through the nature reserve.* Castro Marim itself can be seen ahead. The start of Walk 20 is on the left, 1.6km from the roundabout on the N125. Turn left into **Castro Marim**★ (57km ♁■▬WC),

*A Reserve Centre (*i*) has opened on the banks of the Guadiana River. To get there, continue north on the N122, going under the motorway. Take the first turning right (signposted 'Reserva Natural'), then turn right again, back under the motorway. The centre is the huge brown building down the track/road to the left. The Castro Marim Reserve, around the Reserve Centre, is a good location for bird watching. There is a board outside the centre showing short walks, and leaflets are available inside. The centre closes from 12.30 to 14.00.

and park in the car park. The castle entrance is up to the right. There are photographs of the area on pages 125 and 128. Castro Marim is one of the best areas for bird-watching in Algarve; see notes for Walk 20 on page 125.

Leave Castro Marim along the N125-6 in the direction of Tavira. At the point where a fork goes off right to 'Rio Seco' (59km), keep round to the left. Go over a level crossing (62km) and meet the N125 after 64km, where you turn right in the direction of Faro. Keep on the N125 as far as the high level bridge at Tavira (about 3km after the Eurotel complex on the right), and turn right on the N397 towards Cachopo (81km). Keep right at the 'Picota'

Unknown Algarve: these gloriously green rolling hills lie between Tavira and Cachopo.

Farmhouse on the road between Tavira and Cachopo

sign. The road initially crosses a plain, with the river on the left, heading towards the hills.

Eucalyptus trees line the road as it starts to climb, passing the occasional vineyard and olive grove. Uniformly-rounded hills roll into the distance as you penetrate this unknown but extremely photogenic area of Algarve (📷). A delightful and unusual mosaic, created by varying shades of vegetative cover, cloaks the landscape (📷), adding a delicious hint of unreality and adventure. After 111km, you start to descend, to pass a café and cross the Ribeira de Odeleite. The changing scene is coloured by clusters of pink heather, *Erica australis,* as you pass a fountain on the right (115km). Just when you begin to feel really isolated and in the middle of nowhere, terraced hillsides, cleared of *matos,* announce the proximity of habitation. **Cachopo** (121km ✝✕⬛) is reached just after you pass an impressive cemetery on the right. Stretch your legs and explore this interesting backwater.

Leave Cachopo by turning left on the N124 towards Barranco do Velho; after 1km look out for a picturesque old stone bridge on the left. The road now winds along at a high level (📷) through the pleasant rural hamlets of **Catraia** and **Feiteira** to Barranco do Velho. There is a windmill on the left (137km), before you start to descend into forest. When you reach **Barranco do Velho** (145km ▲▲✕⬛), the N124 goes off right towards Alte and São Bartolomeu de Messines, but keep round left on the N2, to plunge down into the forest towards São Brás and Faro.

On reaching **São Brás de Alportel** (158km ✝▲▲▲✕⊕

THE BARRIER ISLANDS

There is a group of islands and sand banks lying offshore in the general area south and east of Faro and, if you fly into Faro airport, you will have an excellent overall view of them as you start to descend. The whole of this area is a nature reserve called 'Parque Natural da Ria Formosa'. The outermost islands are known as the 'barrier islands', since they protect the inland side from the worst of the rough seas, particularly when the Atlantic breakers are in full swell.

Two of the islands in the central area are popular for bathing. Both are reached by regular ferry from Olhão. The nearest, Ilha de Armona, is reached in about 15 minutes by ferry, and it is almost pure sand. The beach on the sheltered side runs into shallow, warm waters; it is an ideal family beach. The seaward side offers the longer beach, stretching almost all the way to Tavira. This means that you can almost always find a quiet spot of your own.

The second island, Ilha da Culatra, is reached after a 45-minute ferry ride and has permanent habitation. Although just as beautiful, this island is generally less visited because of the longer ferry journey. Full details of the boat timetables are available from the tourist office in Olhão and from the ticket kiosk on the harbour.

Ilha de Armona is also accessible from Tavira. Frequent buses run from the square, Praça da Republica, and travel along the coast to connect up with the ferry, which runs constantly throughout the day in the season. This eastern end of the island has more facilities and is perhaps a little more crowded. Again, the inland side is well sheltered, and the seaward side enjoys the full force of the Atlantic.

The most easterly of these barrier islands, Cabanas, can be reached from the town of Cabanas just to the east of Tavira.

WC*P*18; Walk 18), keep ahead for Faro. If you wish to stop in São Brás, turn left towards the centre *(centro)* and park there, or take the next left turn out of the square, into the main shopping street to park. See the notes for Walk 18 on page 117 for more information about São Brás.

From São Brás, swiftly descend onto the plain, first passing the point where Walk 17 crosses the road on its return (162km), and then passing the left turn to Estói. Walk 17 crosses the road here (165km), on its outward route. You regain **Faro** after 175km.

Orange groves on the drive up to Monte São Miguel

MONTE SÃO MIGUEL

Standing alone on the eastern side of Faro, this mound is a landmark which can be seen for miles around. It would be easy to identify even without the TV transmitter perched on the summit. It's not its height (only 410m/1345ft), but the fact that it stands on the edge of a large area of plain, that makes it so visible. Conversely, it is a good viewpoint, the best in the east. It doesn't offer anything in the way of walking possibilities, but it is worth the drive up to enjoy the views, if you are in the region.

Perhaps you could combine this excursion with a visit to the Sunday market at Moncarapacho (see 'Country fairs and markets' on page 17). Moncarapacho lies 7km north of the N125 (to the northwest of Olhão).

Start out for São Miguel from Moncarapacho by heading north towards Santa Catarina. After about 1km, fork left into a narrow surfaced road (where there is a hard-to-read signpost for São Miguel). This road leads over the motorway all the way up to the summit after 5km, but be sure to keep left at the fork near the top. Apart from good views, there are some interesting wild flowers to be seen, if you make short forays into the *matos*.

5 MÉRTOLA CIRCUIT

Faro • Santana da Serra • Almodôvar • Mértola • Castro Marim • Faro

287km/178mi; about 5h driving.

En route: Walk 20

The outward drive uses the fast route into Alentejo via the A22 motorway across Algarve and then the A2 (toll) Lisbon motorway, but later cuts across the very different Alentejana countryside to reach Mértola. There are one or two recommended stops mentioned in the text. The southerly return route follows the line of the Guadiana through pastoral countryside back to the eastern side of Algarve. Alternatively use the slower IC1 road north (see footnote).

Continuously occupied for more than 2000 years, layers of history are rarely so transparent as at Mértola on the banks of the Guadiana River. This historic walled town has a Roman port in a remarkable state of preservation, a castle, a mosque converted into a church and several fine museums (free entry). Located in Alentejo close to the border with Algarve, Mértola is a little-visited town in spite of its powerful attractions. The authors' guide is strongly recommended to get the most out of this visit (see 'Background reading' on page 6). There are good restaurants in the town, and it is worth considering an overnight stop to explore the region's other places of interest.

Leave Faro by heading north, to pick up the A22 motorway at Junction 13 or 14, where you turn left. When you reach the intersection with the northbound A2 at Junction 10/15 (45km), follow signs for Lisbon.* Collect a ticket at the toll booth, then motor steadily north, to exit at Junction 13, signposted to Almodôvar. Turn left at the roundabout for Mértola. **Gomes Aires** (108km 🏍) lies just to the right. Beyond this village you have a taste of typical Alentejana landscape — rolling tracts of land dotted with umberella-shaped oak trees, providing summer shade for the pigs. (There is an excellent folk museum at Santa Clara-a-Nova: to get there, take a short detour off to the right. The museum is often locked but will be opened on demand — just ask.) **Almodôvar** (118.5km 🏍✕🏍🏍M) is larger than expected, but the N267 to Mértola is well

*To avoid the motorway, stay on the A22 to Junction 9, then take the IC1 (old IP1) north. This slower route is about the same distance. Keep alert on approaching Santana da Serra (93.5km), note the junction with a turning left to Santa Clara and, just 1km further on the IC1, at the top of the hill, turn right into a narrow surfaced road signposted to Almodôvar. Just 0.6km further on, turn right again on the N393. Gomes Aires is soon reached, where you join the A2 (toll) motorway route of the main tour. Follow the main tour from the 108km-point to continue.

signposted — even though the route weaves through the town.

More open countryside follows, but at 138km there is a chance for another short diversion on the right — into São Miguel do Pinheiro, to see a restored, working windmill busy producing flour. Bread is baked here in faithfully-restored ovens and sold in the shop. There is a coffee shop and restaurant close by.

The atmospheric old walls of **Mértola** (160km ⏸🛏⛪ ✕☕🍴M) only appear once you are close to the town. There is a car park on the left, from whe]re it's just a short walk up to the right into the compact centre. The tourist office is a good first stop, to see if the museums are open (some just open on demand out of the main season). Apart from the highlights mentioned on page 39, the Roman museum is worth a visit. It occupies the excavated remains of a Roman villa beneath the town hall. (There

Mértola

are no signs of it until you enter the main town hall door, from where you walk down to the lower level.)

Leave by the same road and fork left on the N122 after 2.5km, following signs to Vila Real. More engaging open countryside fills the windscreen, with just one or two small villages to add variety. Pick up the IC27 from Santa Marta, and you soon reach the **Alcoutim/Cachopo junction** (188km), where you have a choice of routes. The main tour continues straight ahead on the IC27 to **Castro Marim** (Walk 20) and **Vila Real**, where you join the A22 motorway (228.5km). Head back west to Junction 14 and **Faro** (287km).

But the run alongside the Guadiana River and the Spanish border, via Alcoutim, is very scenic and recommended if time allows. It is a little slower and adds around 8km to the tour.

A third route, back to central Algarve via Cachopo and Barranco do Velho (see Car tour 4), is also scenic, but very slow going.

O CCUPYING A DOMINANT POSITION on the once-navigable Guadiana River, Mértola enjoyed a long period of prosperity from Roman times right through into the 13th century. Under Islamic rule, Mértola was twice capital of a kingdom which included Beja. Echoes of the past are inescapable; every street, every corner has a story to tell.

The best place to start is the castle which crowns the hill. On the way up it is often possible to look inside the church where the *mirhab* is still visible behind the altar. Note the Moorish arch of the side door. Within the castle grounds there are ongoing excavations, where a huge cryptoporticum has been slowly and painfully excavated. Enquire at the tourist office about guided tours which are run twice-daily when there is demand.

The Roman museum is exceptionally well presented within the excavated remains of a Roman villa beneath the town hall. Showcases set amongst the ruins themselves display some of the finds. The Museum of Islamic Art has the finest display of Islamic pottery in Portugal. No doubt the storks' nests will still be resident on the clock tower nearby, and there are good views down over the Roman port at this point.

Just 17km east of Mértola lies the Mina de São Domingos. Once worked by the Romans, this huge copper and sulphur mine was run by a British company for over a hundred years before it closed in 1965. A narrow-gauge railway transported the copper and sulphur south to Pomarão, from where it was shipped down-river to Vila Real. The mine is now a museum with an on-site hotel.

The cork oak (bottom) is an important feature of the Algarve landscape. The cork collection point shown at the left is encountered at the 35min-point in Walk 7.

● Walking

Algarve is justly famous for its fine beaches and beautiful coastline. It is not normally thought of in terms of open countryside, pretty villages and ideal rambling opportunities. Many visitors will be surprised by the fine and varied landscapes to be enjoyed across the length of the region. To the north and east, the rolling, interlocking *matos*-covered hills catch the long rays of the sun, to present an ever-changing interplay of light and shade. The limestone of the central Barrocal plays host to most of the charming villages — and to the best of the wild flowers. Further west, the granite mountains of the Serra de Monchique provide the ruggedness and grandeur. Further west still, the landscape takes on a windswept appearance, which is at its most extreme as you approach Sagres. It is impossible to ignore the fine coastline, and we have made the most of those parts which are still unspoilt, so that you can enjoy some of the scenery which has contributed to the fame of this beautiful region.

There are enough walks to fill the whole of a two-week holiday and to tempt you back for more. The groundwork has been done, so from day one you can be out in the countryside, enjoying your holiday to the full. But please accept some words of caution. Follow the walks as described, and never try to get from one walk to another across uncharted terrain — even though it may look possible. Promising-looking tracks or paths may only lead to someone's smallholding, and distances can be very deceptive in the high hills and across coastal gullies.

Locals no longer use many of the routes, sections of which are in danger of becoming overgrown. We spend time chopping back foliage when we are in Algarve and would be grateful if other wielders of secateurs made the odd snip here and there to help keep routes open for everyone. Thank you to those of you who already do!

There are walks in this book for everyone. All walks are graded, so just check the grade to see if it suits you and, if the grade of the main walk is too advanced, be sure to check all the shorter versions.

If you are an inexperienced walker, or if you are just looking for a gentle walk, then go for the walks graded 'easy'. Try perhaps the coastal walks, where you can go only as far as you like, before returning. Look too at the picnic suggestions on pages 8-13, which visit a selection of particularly beautiful spots — many of which are easily reached in under an hour's walking.

Experienced walkers should be able to tackle all of the walks in this book, dependent on the season and the weather conditions. If a walk is very long, do be sure of your fitness before you attempt it. Don't attempt the more strenuous walks in high summer; do protect yourself from the sun, and always carry an ample supply of water and plenty of fruit. Always remember that storm damage could make some of the walks described in this book unsafe, so be sure to err on the side of safety. If you have not reached one of our landmarks after a reasonable time, then you must return to the last 'sure' point and start again.

For **expert walkers**, the walks around Monchique offer the best challenge and, if you are out to test your stamina, it is possible to join some walks together to make a longer day.

Guides, waymarking, maps

Official **guides** are not available, but none is needed for the walks in this book. Most of the walks use well established footpaths, trails and tracks, and are easily followed.

Waymarks are seen along some of the walks but, generally, these are not helpful. In some areas coloured arrows painted on walls are used to show the way to houses which are off the beaten track. To avoid any possible confusion, it is wiser to follow our directions at all times, in preference to any route markings.

The **maps** in this book are adapted from the 1:50,000 maps produced since the 1960s by the Instituto Geográfico e Cadastral. These are the latest maps available, but they are very outdated.* We have improved them by adding roads and some *major* tracks. But at this scale it is impossible to include the myriad of footpaths and minor tracks in the region. Used in conjunction with the walking notes, however, the maps provide a helpful overview of the walks, clearly indicating the general direction and the surrounding terrain.

---

*There are also 1:25,000 maps of Algarve available, published from the 1960s to the 1990s. Although they show more detail, they are generally as outdated as the smaller-scale maps, since there has been a tremendous amount of road- and track-building during the 1990s.

What to take

If you are already in Portugal when you find this book, and you haven't any special equipment such as a rucksack and walking boots, you can still do some of the walks — but better still, buy some of the equipment you need locally. Boots, shoes, and trainers can all be bought fairly cheaply, provided you do not require a large size. Continental size 45 is often the upper limit for men and 41 for women. Don't attempt any of the difficult walks without the proper gear or with brand-new footwear. Always check the *grade of the walk:* if it is easy and follows fairly level tracks or footpaths, you should be able to wear trainers. (Do *not* wear sandals, as explained under 'Things that bite or sting' below.) If we mention loose-stone paths or steep descents, then walking boots are absolutely essential; you will need to rely on the grip and ankle support they provide. All other walks should be made with stout shoes, preferably with thick rubber soles to grip on wet and slippery surfaces. You may find the following check list useful:

walking boots (which must be broken-in) and spare boot laces
waterproof rain gear (outside summer months)
long-sleeved shirt (for sun protection)
long trousers, tight at the ankles (sun and tick protection)
plastic groundsheet
antiseptic cream
woollen hat and gloves
water bottle with water purifying tablets
'Dog Dazer' (see page 47)
secateurs (see page 43)

swimming costume
bandages and band aids
plastic plates, cups, etc
knives and openers
anorak (zip opening)
sunhat, sunglasses, suncrean
universal sink plug
insect repellent
binoculars
two cardigans
extra pair (long) socks
compass, whistle, torch
small rucksack
compact folding umbrella (also useful as a sun-shade)

Please bear in mind that we have not done *every* walk in the book under *all* conditions. We might not realise just how hot or exposed some walks might be in high summer or how cold in winter. For this reason we have listed above all the gear you *might* need, depending on the season, and we rely on your good judgement to modify the list accordingly.

Beware of the sun and the effects of dehydration. Don't be deceived by light cloud cover; you can still get sunburnt. While it's tempting to wear shorts for walking, always carry long trousers and a long-sleeved shirt and put them on when you have had enough sun — and *always* wear a sunhat. Don't forget that, with the sun behind you, the backs of your legs and your neck are getting badly sunburnt. (Pushing through prickly holly oak in shorts isn't much fun either.) Choose a shady spot for your lunch on hot days, and make sure that you carry with you a good supply of fruit and water.

W here to stay

There is a wide range of resorts to suit all tastes in Algarve, most of them situated along the coast. Those who prefer a more **rural atmosphere** will find a growing choice of accommodation inland, particularly in the area between **Silves** and **São Brás de Alportel** and around **Monchique**.

The **central part of the coastline** is also a good area in which to stay, because you can get to most parts of Algarve without too much travelling. **Albufeira** is the largest resort in this region, and has good bus connections, although it is not so convenient for trains. The nearest station is at Ferreira, 6km outside the resort. For a quieter place to stay, try some of the smaller places outside Albufeira like **Montechoro**. It makes a central base for walkers with a hire car and allows for easy escapes into the countryside.

Moving **westwards, Carvoeira** is a lively resort and **Alvor**, near **Portimão**, has grown apace. If you prefer small, quieter places, then look west of Lagos now, although this region is already being developed at an alarming rate. **Lagos** is a pleasing resort, which seems to combine spaciousness with the peace of somewhere much smaller. Once west of Lagos, the once-quiet resorts are developing rapidly. They are also further away from most of the walks, but the new motorway as far as Lagos has shortened travelling times.

Exploring the **eastern side of the region** is made easier from the central resorts by the motorway. **Faro** does have hotels and is a convenient centre for public transport, but does not have the traditional image of a resort. **Olhão**, to the east of Faro, is even less easy on the eye, but convenient for boats out to the beautiful beaches of the barrier islands. **Tavira**, possibly the most picturesque resort on the easturn side, is also a centre for boat trips out to the barrier islands. **Monte Gordo**, almost on the eastern border with Spain, is also a popular resort, but from here few of the walks are within easy reach.

Weather

The kindest months for walking in this part of Portugal are those either side of summer: March, April, May, September and October. However, walking through the mild winter months can be entirely delightful. There are likely to be many fine days, even in January, which are quite superb for walking. February, too, can provide many good opportunities and be the equal of any of the later spring months. By March the temperature is starting to rise, and it is certainly warm enough to air the shorts. Sunny days are plentiful, but there is still a chance of a day or two with rain, and these conditions prevail through April, even though the temperature is increasing steadily. May brings more warmth and sunshine, with only a small risk of unsettled weather. By June the weather is getting too hot for strenuous walks, but some of the coastal walks, where you will be cooled by the Atlantic sea breezes, can still be enjoyed — as they can throughout the summer months.

As the summer heat starts to decline in September, a new walking season opens up. This lasts through October and into November — until the start of the rainy season. The late autumn is often the wettest part of the year, but the average annual rainfall for the area, especially the coastal region, is very low, at 400-500mm (16-20 inches). *Be aware that after heavy rain, walks which cross rivers (16, 18, 19) may be impassable for a few days; Walk 20 will be sticky, slippery mud.*

Things that bite or sting

Dogs can be a nuisance. We were thankful to be carrying a 'Dog Dazer', which we found to be very effective, and it gave us considerable confidence. A Dog Dazer is a small, easily-portable electronic device which, on the press of a button, emits a noise which is inaudible to the human ear, but which startles aggressive dogs and persuades them to back off. For information about the Dog Dazer, contact Sunflower Books, who sell them. Otherwise, the best advice, if you feel threatened and have no walking stick, is to pick up a stone and pretend to throw it. More often than not, the dogs bark loudly but are rarely actually aggressive.

Snakes are something you will have to be on your guard against. We see very few in winter or spring, but we are advised that there are more around in summer.

Most are probably harmless, but if there are any of the viper species around, then great care is needed. Most snakes are more frightened of you than you are of them, and they will move out of your way rapidly. But, if they don't, the best advice is to move quietly out of their way. The real danger comes should you accidentally step on a snake. For this reason, it is *imperative* that you do not walk in the countryside in open sandals, no matter how comfortable they might be for walking. Always have your feet and ankles well covered. It is also a sensible precaution to wear your long trousers tucked into your socks. Take special care near water, when you are about to sit down, or when you choose to rest your hand, so unthinkingly, on a dry-stone wall.

Scorpions are around, too, most likely seen in the height of summer, when they are usually seeking shade — so don't leave any of your clothing on the ground. Accidentally turning over rocks or stones may expose them but, generally, they offer no serious threat, since their sting is more painful than dangerous for most people.

In areas which are well forested, **ticks** can be a problem. As you brush through the woodlands, they can get onto your clothes. Again, if you follow our advice about wearing long trousers and a long-sleeved shirt, you should be able to keep them off your skin. If they do manage to get to your skin, then it is necessary to make them withdraw before you take them off. An easy way to do this is to touch them with a solvent such as methylated spirits or petrol.

Bees and **wasps** are around in summer, so make sure you carry the necessary creams and pills, especially if you are allergic to insect bites.

H unting season

The hunting season lasts from October to January with shooting allowed on Sundays, Thursdays and Public Holidays. Walkers in the countryside should be aware of possible personal danger on these days.

A country code for walkers and motorists

The experienced rambler is used to following a 'country code', but the tourist out for a lark may unwittingly cause damage, harm animals, and even endanger his own life. Do heed this advice:

- **Do not light fires**; everything gets tinder-dry in summer. Stub out cigarettes with care.

- **Do not frighten animals**. The goats and sheep you may encounter on your walks are not tame. By making loud noises or trying to touch them or photograph them, you may cause them to run in fear and be hurt.
- **Walk quietly** through all farms, hamlets and villages, leaving all gates just as you found them. Gates do have a purpose, usually to keep animals in (or out of) an area. Remember, too, that a gate may be of a temporary nature — brushwood across the path — but it serves the same purpose, so please replace it after passing.
- **Protect all wild and cultivated plants**. Don't try to pick wild flowers or uproot saplings. They will die before you even get back to the hotel. When photographing wild flowers, watch where you put your feet so that you do not destroy others in the process. Obviously fruit and crops are someone's private property and should not be touched.
- **Never walk over cultivated land**.
- **Take all your litter away with you**.
- **Walkers — do not take risks**. Do not attempt walks beyond your capacity and **never** walk alone. *Always* tell a responsible person *exactly* where you are going and what time you plan to return. Remember, if you become lost or injure yourself, it may be a long time before you are found. On any but a very short walk near villages, it's a good idea to take along a torch, a whistle, a compass, extra water and warm clothing — as well as some high-energy food like chocolate. Review the 'Important note to the reader' on page 2 and the 'Walkers' checklist' on page 51.

Walk 5: Pé do Frio — just a loose scattering of houses

Portuguese for walkers

Despite the large numbers of tourists visiting Algarve, British tourists in particular, we found surprisingly little English spoken outside the major resorts. To ask directions in the countryside, you may well need to try your hand at Portuguese. A good technique is to memorise a few key questions, and then try to phrase your question so that it demands a 'yes' (*sim;* pronounced **seng**) or 'no' (*não;* pronounced **nowg**) answer. It is not always possible to conduct the whole conversation in this manner, so it pays to learn a few other answers that you might expect, or which you can use to form more questions to get yes/no answers. Examples of key questions and possible answers are given below.

Key questions

English	Portuguese	approximate pronunciation
'Pardon me,	Faz o favor,	Fahz oh fah-**vohr**,
sir (madam).	senhor (senhora).	sehn-**yohr** (sehn-**yoh**-rah).
Where is	Onde é	**Ohn**-deh eh
the footpath to ...	a vereda para ...	ah veh-**ray**-dah **pah**-rah ...
(the road to	(a estrada para ...	(ah ish-**trah**-dah **pah**-rah
the way to... ...	o caminho para ...	oh cah-**mee**-noh **pah**-rah
the bus stop)?	a paragem)?	ah pah-**rah**-jeng?
Many thanks.'	Muito obrigado.	**Mween**-toh oh-bree-**gah**-doh
	(a woman says muito obrigada).	(oh-bree-**gah**-dah).

Possible answers

English	Portuguese	approximate pronunciation
here	aqui	ah-**key**
there	ali	ah-**lee**
straight ahead	sempre em frente	**sem**-preh em **frenght**
behind	atrás	ah-**trahsh**
to the right	a dereita	ah deh-**ray**-tah
to the left	a esquerda	ah ish-**kehr**-dah
above	em cima	engh **see**-mah
below	em baixo	engh **bigh**-joh

Try to get a native speaker (possibly somebody at the hotel or a taxi driver) to help you learn the pronunciation. You must pronounce the name of your destination *very carefully*. For guidance with the pronunciation of place names mentioned in this book, see the Index, beginning on page 133.)

When you have your mini-speech memorised, always ask the many questions that you can concoct from it in such a way that a yes/no answer will result. *Never* ask an open-ended question such as 'Where is the main road?' and leave it at that! Unless you are actually standing on it, you will not understand the answer! Instead, ask the question and then suggest the most likely answer yourself, for example:

'Faz o favor, senhora. Onde é a estrada para Faro? É sempre em frente?' or 'Faz o favor, senhor. Onde é a verada para Alte? É em cima a esquerda?'

If you go through your list of answers, you will eventually get a yes — with a vigorous nod of the head — and it will be a lot more reliable than sign language.

An inexpensive phrase book is a very valuable aid from which you can choose other 'key' phrases and answers. Remember, too, that it is always pleasant to greet people you may meet on your walks with a 'good morning' (bom dia/bohm **dee**-ah) or 'good afternoon' (boa tarde/boah **tard**).

Walkers' checklist
The following points cannot be stressed too often:

- **At any time a walk may become unsafe** due to storms or bulldozing. If the route is not as we describe it, and your way ahead is not secure, *do not attempt to go on.*
- **Never walk alone** — four is the best walking group.
- **Do not overestimate your energies** — your pace will be determined by the slowest walker in the group.
- **Transport** connections at the end of the walk are very important.
- Proper **footwear** and **sun protection** are mandatory.
- **Mists** can suddenly appear in the mountains.
- **Warm clothing** is needed in the mountains; even in summer, take some along, in case you are delayed.
- **Compass, whistle, torch, first-aid kit** weigh little, but might save your life.
- **Extra rations** must be taken on long walks.
- A **stout stick** is a help on rough terrain and to discourage the rare unchained, menacing dog.
- **Review** the 'Important note' on page 2, as well as grade and equipment for each walk, before you set out.

Organisation of the walks
The twenty major walks in this book are spread across the whole of Algarve, with the greatest concentration around the central area. Begin by considering the large fold-out touring map inside the back cover. Here you can see the overall terrain, the road network, and the

position of the walking maps in the book. Flipping through the pages, you will find that there is at least one photograph for each walk.

Having selected potential excursions from the map and photographs, look over the planning information at the beginning of each walk to find distance/walking time, grade, and how to get there and return. If the grade is beyond your scope, don't despair! There's almost always a short or alternative version of the walk and, in most cases, these are less demanding of ability and equipment. If it still looks too strenuous for you, turn to pages 8-13, where the picnic suggestions allow you to savour a walk's special landscape with the minimum of effort.

The text of the walk begins with an introduction to give you a flavour of the landscape and comments about special points of interest, before the route is described in detail. The text is illustrated with 1:50,000 maps (all with north at the top). These have been overprinted with the routes and key landmarks; see under 'Guides, waymarking, maps' on page 44.

Note that **we are fairly fit walkers** and that our time checks include only brief pauses, where you might stop to recover breath. They do *not* include photographic or picnic stops — or any stops of indeterminate length. **It is *not* intended that you match these frequent time-checks throughout the walk**; they are given to indicate the *time difference* from one point to another (and to facilitate reference to the short and alternative walks). This means that *you should allow up to twice as long as the stated time*. Don't forget to take bus connections at the end of the walk into account, particularly with regard to the last bus of the day. The most important factor is *consistency* of walking times, and we have made an effort to check our times at least twice. You'll soon see how your pace compares with ours and make adjustments for your stride … and the heat!

Below is a key to the **symbols** on the walking maps:

▬▬▬	motorway	♦ †	church.cross
▬▬▬	primary road	▪ ⛫	castle or fort.ancient site
▬▬▬	secondary road	✿ ⚒	mill.windmill
▬▬▬	minor road	🚗 🚌	car parking.bus stop
▬▬▬	track	🚃	railway station
-----	footpath	♪	spring *(fonte)* or well
⋯3→	walking route and direction	P	picnic spot (pages 8-13)
⋯3→	alternative route	∪⚒	lime kiln.quarry
⋯200⋯	height (m)	☞	best views

1 LUZ • *ATALAIA* • PORTO DE MÓS • PONTA DA PIEDADE • LAGOS

See also photographs pages 1, 6, 25

Distance: 9.6km/6mi; just over 2h

Grade: easy-moderate. The walk is mainly on footpaths, with some climbing involved, especially in the first part from Luz to the obelisk *(atalaia)* at 109m/358ft.

Equipment: See pages 44-45.

How to get there: 🚌 by bus from Lagos to Luz (Timetable 1). Journey time 15min. 🚗 by car: immediately on entering Luz follow the sign 'Praia da Luz' off left, down to a car park by the sea front. If you do arrive by car, the chances are that you will have to walk back the same way: see Alternative walk 4 below.

Short walks: Both are easy.

1 Luz — *atalaia* — Luz (2.8km/1.75mi; 36min; a stiff climb). Follow the start of the walk to the obelisk *(atalaia)* and return the same way.

2 Luz — Porto de Mós — Luz (8.8km/5.5mi; 1h50min). Follow the main walk for 53min, and make this your turning point. There are café/bars where you can take refreshments before returning. The beach is stony close to the path, but sandy further out.

Alternative walks

3 Luz — Ponta da Piedade — Luz (12.8km/8mi; 2h45min). Follow the main walk to the lighthouse; return the same way. Easy-moderate.

4 Luz — Lagos — Luz (18.6km/11.5mi; 4h). If you go by car, you may have to walk back the same way, because of the limited bus services between Lagos and Luz (Timetable 1). Easy-moderate.

Burgau (Longer walk 1-6 and Walks 2 and 3) is one of the Algarvian fishing villages that has retained its character despite all the touristic development further east along the splendid coast.

5   Porto de Mós — Ponta da Piedade — Porto de Mós (4.0km/2.5mi; 1h). This option is available only if you are travelling by car or taxi. Park in the large car park at Porto de Mós: on approaching Lagos from Portimão, immediately after crossing the bridge turn left at the roundabout and follow signs for Sagres. Negotiate the next three roundabouts by going right, left, right. Then keep ahead uphill to another roundabout, where Luz and Sagres are signposted to the right. Turn left here, and then turn right 1.4km further on, following the sign to Porto de Mós (2km). Walk from the car park to the lighthouse at Ponta da Piedade, following the main walk from the 53min-point); return the same way.

Longer walks: The coastal footpath stretches all the way from Lagos to Salema. We have broken the route down into three stretches which are presented as Walks 1-3. All the sections have a totally different character with different points of interest and, if you want to spend a little time on the various beaches, exploring the villages or relaxing in the café/bars, then they are worth doing separately. But they can be joined together in various combinations — as follows. See map pages 60-61.

6   Salema to Luz via Burgau (10.1km/6.3mi; 2h40min). Taxi or bus to Salema (Timetable 2) and walk back to Luz using the map on pages 60-61 (Walk 3 and then Walk 2, both in reverse). Return from Luz by bus (Timetable 1).

7   Burgau to Lagos via Luz (14km/8.7mi; 3h10min). Take a bus out to Burgau, as in Walk 3, and walk back to Lagos, using the map on pages 60-61 to walk to Luz (Walk 2 in reverse). Then pick up Walk 1.

8   Salema to Lagos (19.5km/12.1mi; 4h40min). Take a taxi or bus out to Salema (Timetable 2) and walk the whole distance back to Lagos. Use the map on pages 60-61 as far as Luz, then pick up Walk 1.

Coastal footpaths always have great appeal, and this one is no exception. The moods of the sea, the play of light, a weaving coastline, the tang of salt, and secluded bays all help to etch them firmly into the memory. Fine views from the obelisk *(atalaia)* above Luz are one of the highlights of this walk, as is the lighthouse and the egretry at Ponta da Piedade. The interest at this point is the spectacular rugged coastline and the stacks around the coast (see photograph page 56).

Luz itself was a relatively small fishing village lying to the west of Lagos, but is rapidly developing as a tourist resort. The old

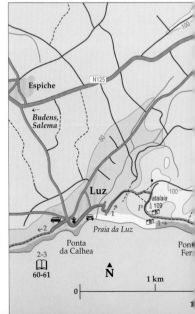

centre is still intact, with some good restaurants and cafés. There are some fine beaches where you can swim or enjoy water sports such as windsurfing.

Interesting wild flowers, including orchids, can be found all along this part of the coast, and a description of these is given in the panel on page 59.

Start the walk from the CAR PARK by the sea at the eastern side of **Luz**: turn left towards the obelisk that you can see on the headland. Follow the cobbled road to the T-junction reached in under **1min**, where you turn right. At the second T-junction, a minute later, turn left, away from the shore. As the cobbled road ends, stay ahead on the rough track and follow it up the hillside. After **6min**, the track is leading you towards the obelisk, and you can see a path heading directly up the steepest part of the hillside. It is better *not* to take this path, but to use the curving path to the left. Erosion has made the footpaths difficult in parts, so some care is needed. The slow ascent at least gives you time to scan the hillside for flowers before you reach the OBELISK (*'atalaia'* on the map; Picnic 1; **20min**).

From the *atalaia* there are some fine views to enjoy over Luz and along the coast, as well as along the valley inland. Continue from here by following the track past the obelisk, heading in the direction of Lagos. The track dips through a hollow (**21min**), and back to the cliff tops. The walking soon becomes fairly level for a time, at a height of about 75m/250ft, and you gain views of Lagos ahead

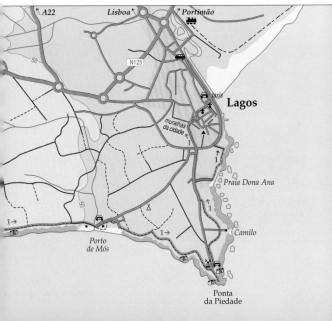

Ponta da Piedade

— as well as the lighthouse. Then you start the descent to Porto de Mós (**48min**), continuing ahead and taking care on this badly eroded track.

There is a selection of restaurant/cafés at **Porto de Mós** (**53min**) or an opportunity to picnic on the beach. To continue, head for the far side of the bay and the road out to Lagos. Walk up the road for about 6 minutes, until the wall of the complex on the right ends, and take the cobbled track off right. On meeting crossroads a minute later, turn left uphill. Shortly, where a road goes left, climb up the low wall on the right, onto a road. Stay ahead for a few minutes, and you will come to a turning and parking area at the edge of the cliff. To the left of the wall ahead, you can pick up the coastal path again (**1h08min**). Now the path undulates slightly, before you reach the LIGHT-HOUSE at **Ponta da Piedade** (**1h25min**).

Beyond the lighthouse, good views can be had if you have the energy to descend the steps to the landing stage, where boat trips from Praia Dona Ana land their passengers. Look carefully at the various stacks to identify the one used by the egrets as their breeding ground. It came as a surprise and delight to us to find that there are still regions of Algarve which remain unspoilt and where fine coastal walks are possible. Another such walk, further east, is described in Walk 10.

The final stage into Lagos is mainly road walking. Continue around the lighthouse to the CAR PARK (**1h27min**; restaurant/bar in season). Follow the Lagos road past the car park; then take the path on the right (**1h29min**). It wanders a little away from the road, to cross another road (**1h37min**) near a restaurant on the right above the beach at **Camilo**. From here it heads diagonally back to the Lagos road across a rocky, sandy area, rejoining it through GATEPOSTS (**1h41min**). Turn right here. Keep ahead at the junction (**1h43min**; but divert right if you want to see the small resort and lovely beach at Praia Dona Ana, shown on page 6, and perhaps follow the coastal path to Lagos). You swing right through the CITY WALLS ten minutes later. Follow the one-way system through the old town, turning left at the traffic lights (**1h58min**). The MAIN SQUARE at **Lagos** (PRAÇA GIL EANES) comes into view five minutes later (**2h03min**). The bus stops alongside the riverside road; the BUS STATION is upriver, opposite the marina.

A typical tiled façade in Lagos

See also photograph page 53

Distance: 9.5km/5.9mi; 2h10min

Grade: easy. There is only one significant climb over a headland, and the footpaths, although stony in parts, are mostly good.

Equipment: See pages 44-45.

How to get there: 🚌 by bus from Lagos to Luz (Timetable 1). Journey time 15min. 🚗 by car: Immediately on entering Luz, follow the sign off left to Praia da Luz, to descend to a car park by the sea front.
To return: 🚌 from Luz to Lagos (Timetable 1), or 🚗 car

Short walk: Luz to Burgau (4.7km/2.9mi; 1h05min; grade as main walk). Follow the notes for the main walk to Burgau. Return from Burgau to Lagos by 🚌 bus (Timetable 1). Journey time 22min.

Longer walk: See Walk 1 for details of longer walks, including the option of walking between Luz and Salema.

This section of coastal path, westwards from Luz, is the easiest and the shortest. Although there are no sandy bays en route, Burgau awaits you, with its long stretch of beach — fine for swimming or just relaxing. See Walks 1 and 3 for more about the villages of Luz and Burgau.

Start the walk from the CAR PARK at the sea front on the eastern side of **Luz**. Set out westward, away from the obelisk, along the PROMENADE. Turn right at the end of the promenade to pass a CHURCH on your right (**5min**) and then, almost immediately, take the first road left. This

About 40 minutes into the walk. Note the Agave americana in the foreground. This plant was introduced into the Mediterranean area from Mexico over two centuries ago. Now it is widely naturalised — even on the southwestern Atlantic coast.

sets you heading towards the open country. The road runs into track and, when the track swings right 10 minutes later, take the path down left along the seashore.

Be sure to watch out and avoid some DEEP HOLES on the right (**19min**). From here the path leads you left around a raised flat area, to end up at a slightly higher level (**23min**). As you reach a deep rocky bay (**26min**), cut inland to round it, keeping to the seaward side of the villas. Meet a stony stretch of path and follow it to the left. When the stony path turns up right, continue ahead on a path until (**38min**) you are on a path heading up the centre of the hill ahead. (Or you could skirt the base of the hill by taking a path to the right — *not left*.) Looking back, you can see the obelisk at Luz and, beyond it, the lighthouse near Lagos. Close at hand you should find fan-leaved palms and

THERE IS A WEALTH of wild flowers to be found along the whole of this coastal path from Lagos to Salema. Without doubt the best display is in the spring, but many plants, especially the cistus and other shrubs, do have a more prolonged flowering period. Limestone bluffs, eroded valleys offering protection for the plants from the wind and the salt, and deep-red coarse sandy soils are some of the different habitats which are to be seen. Orchids are particularly common in the limestone regions, and the short grass hides many bee orchids, including the bumblebee orchid, *Ophrys bombyliflora*, the yellow bee orchid, *O lutea*, and the mirror orchid, *O speculum* — as well as the tongue orchid, *Serapias parviflora*.

Less common are two charming narcissi — *N bulbocodium*, which resembles a small daffodil (photograph above), and the tiny jonquil, *N gaditanus*. Still on limestone, one interesting plant to see all year round is the dwarf fan palm, *Chamaerops humilis*. This is the only native European palm; it rarely develops a stem, and the flowers are hidden in a dense cluster of leaves. Common all along the cliffs, where it often forms neat mounds, is the yellow-flowered *Asteriscus maritimus*, which belongs to the daisy family. Cistus, too, are well represented, with the pink-flowered *Cistus albidus*, the white-flowered sage-leaved cistus, *Cistus salvifolius*, and *Halimium commutatum*, a yellow rock rose. An annual of the same family is the spotted rock rose, *Tuberaria guttata*, which has small yellow flowers with a dark brown centre. The iris are so widespread that they are certain to be noticed — but possibly only after lunch, since *Iris sisyrinchium* opens its flowers only around mid-day. Two more to mention in this short list, both fairly common, are sweet alison, *Lobularia maritima*, with its fragrant small white flowers, and the blue-flowered tassel hyacinth, *Muscari comosum*.

the much taller agaves shown on page 58.

There is a short steep climb now, but new vistas open up as you reach the top (**41min**). Stay clear of the edge, as the cliff is very unstable at this point. Burgau lies on the far side of the windmill which you can see ahead and, on a clear day, it is possible to see all along the coastline to Sagres. Take care on the stony footpath, as you descend to continue on a wide path along the cliff edge.

This clear path leads directly towards Burgau, which you soon enter (**1h**). On reaching a restaurant on the left, the track runs into a road which you follow to descend into the village itself.

As you come into **Burgau (1h03min)**, turn left towards the sea, passing toilets on your right, and continue right along the shore into the fishing harbour.

Return to Luz the same way (**2h10min**) or, to end the Short walk, head up the narrow street from the harbour, to find the BUS STOP.

3 BURGAU • CABANAS VELHAS • BOCA DO RIO • SALEMA • BURGAU

See also photograph page 53   **Distance**: 11km/6.8mi; 3h

Grade: moderate. This coastal walk is full of headlands to negotiate, so there are quite a few ups and downs. Some of the footpaths are stony and can be difficult.

Equipment: See pages 44-45.

How to get there: 🚌 by bus from Lagos to Burgau (Timetable 1). Journey time 22min. 🚗 by car: As you reach Burgau, turn right by the bus shelter into the wide road to park. Don't attempt to take the car down the narrow streets to the sea front.

To return: 🚌 bus from Burgau to Lagos (Timetable 1), or 🚗 car

Short walks

1   Burgau — Ponta da Almádena — Burgau (4.6km/2.9mi; 1h10min). This one is easy, but there is still some climbing and problems with stony paths. Follow the notes for the main walk for the first 35min, until you reach the small sheltered beach at Cabanas Velhas and a café/bar. Return the same way.

2   Burgau — Boca do Rio — Burgau (7.6km/4.7mi; 2h). Moderate. Use the notes for the main walk to go to the beach at Boca do Rio, where there are some Roman remains. Return the same way.

3   Burgau to Salema (5.5km/3.4mi; 1h27min). Moderate. Follow the notes for the main walk all the way to Salema, and return from there by bus to Lagos (Timetable 2). Journey time 32min.

B urgau is one of the few fishing villages in Algarve whose core still retains its charm and character. The main street of the village runs down to the sea, where fishing boats provide plenty of colour. This walk along the cliffs to Salema is very much like travelling a switchback — you climb the bluffs only to descend the other side. The two small beaches encountered en route make good resting places, although the beach at Cabanas Velhas all but disappears at high tide.

The bus stops at the corner of the wide road (near where there is room to park). **Start the walk** from the BUS STOP in **Burgau** by heading west down the wide street with the sea over on your left. In around a minute, just past a WALLED SPORTS AREA, turn left into a narrow road. Follow this round to the right and continue ahead on a cliff path. Skirt the perimeter fence of a complex and wind up to a crossing path (**4min**), where you turn left uphill. Once up on the HEADLAND (**6min**), you enjoy fine views back towards Lagos. The obelisk above Luz and the lighthouse near Lagos can both be seen. Follow the path by the cliff top as it dips down through a hollow. Over to the right farmhouses dot the barren countryside. There is another dip to cross and, as you rise again, the path runs into a rough track (**12min**). Keep ahead on the track by the coast, to get good views of the shingle beaches below. In **25min** you can see Salema ahead and the Sagres headland in the distance. In **29min** the track descends through a cutting, to meet a crossing track a minute later. Turn sharp right here, but turn off this track in under a minute, to descend a path to a small cove at **Cabanas Velhas** (Picnic 3a; **35min**).

Cross the beach to continue, but head towards the sea, to pick up the path that continues along the coast.* There is an initial short steep climb but, by **39min**, you are back on the top again. Ahead you can see an old fort but, before you get there, there is a house to negotiate: as you meet the wall (**40min**), turn down right to keep alongside it and skirt the house (now on your left). Pick up the coastal path

*Following the coast, come to some steps, by a house, in about one minute. The steps are unusable, but a steep path descends alongside them. You may prefer to head inland to the back of the beach and take the track up to the left. This will lead you to the house just beyond the 40min-point.

again beyond here and head towards the fort on the cliff edge. Keep right when there is a choice of paths, and reach the FORT in **50min** (Picnic 3b). Pass through the enclosure and out the other side to continue. Stay with the coastal path as it swings to the right and starts into a steep descent towards the bay of Boca do Rio, lying at the mouth of a flat-bottomed valley. Just before the bottom of the valley (**56min**), the path joins a very rough track by a ruin on the left (note this carefully for the return). Turn left down to the riverside and cross the river on stepping stones at **Boca do Rio** (Picnic 3c). Inland from here is a good area for bird-watching.

The fenced-off area once protected the remains of a Roman settlement, still awaiting excavation. Some of the

Picnics 3b and 3c: looking back towards the fort across the beach at Boca do Rio. Just out of sight, in the foreground, lie some Roman ruins.

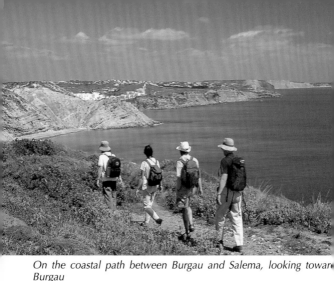

On the coastal path between Burgau and Salema, looking toward Burgau

remains are visible on the shore. The Boca do Rio is under threat of development, including a marina, despite being a conservation area.

Continue on the path leading up the cliff from the beach. Pass round the end of the perimeter fence and join a track at the top of the rise. Keep ahead on this track, following the coast and, when the main track swings inland (**1h11min**), go left on a minor track, then stay left again to continue following the coastline. The photograph on page 63 was taken along this stretch. (An alternative is to keep ahead on the main track and take the next left turn, heading downhill on a surfaced road. Soon fork left into a narrower surfaced road and descend to Salema.)

As you reach the top of a gentle rise, you will see that the track ahead is blocked. Beyond is a house. Go right on a path (at time of writing indicated by a stone arrow and a cairn), and descend to the SALEMA ROAD (**1h20min**). Follow the road down to the seafront at **Salema**, with its beach, restaurants and cafés (**1h27min**). *(To end Short walk 3, catch the bus in the tiny village centre.)*

The main walk returns to **Burgau** the same way (**3h**).

4 FIGUEIRA • INGRINA • ZAVIAL • FIGUEIRA

Distance: 12km/7.5mi; 3h05min

Grade: moderate-strenuous. Moderate undulations and an ascent of some 50m/160ft from Zavial. Some tricky cliff descents. Danger of vertigo on one short stretch during the descent to Praia das Furnas.

Equipment: See pages 44-45.

How to get there and return: 🚌 from Lagos to Figueira (Timetable 2). Journey time 20min. Check bus timetables locally, as more buses call at Budens and Salema than Figueira. The Salema bus turns off the N125 just after Budens, at traffic lights. Alight immediately, where the bus goes left to Salema, and walk the short distance along the road to Figueira. 🚗 by car: travelling from Lagos on the N125, turn left for Salema, but keep ahead immediately for Figueira (as the Salema road goes left). Park on entering Figueira, before the bus shelter and toilets on the left.

Short walk: Figueira — Praia das Furnas — Praia da Figueira — Figueira (6.4km/4mi; 1h40min). Strenuous, with a possibility of vertigo around the 45min-mark). Follow the main walk to the 17min-point and turn left. Now use the map to reach Praia das Furnas (35min). Head to the seaward side of a buttress of rock on the left. To continue, pick up the notes for the Extended walk (below), from the 2h20min-point.

Extended walk: Figueira — Ingrina — Zavial — Praia das Furnas — Praia da Figueira — Figueira (13km/8.1mi; 3h35min). Strenuous, with a possibility of vertigo around the 2h40min-mark. Follow the main walk to the 2h30min-point. Continue across Praia das Furnas, towards a bank of sand on the seaward side of a distinct buttress of rock. Start by taking a few steps up the sand bank, then scramble diagonally uphill to the right across the rough limestone. There is no distinct path, but head up left to the top just before reaching the edge of the cliff. Keep uphill when a cove comes into view ahead. At the top, move inland towards the centre of a saddle in the distance. Then descend diagonally right, to the inland edge of a hollow (2h43min). At this point the sea will be over to your right. Now head up the left flank of the mound ahead and contour round the hillside. Note the track below on the left and, soon, where a track leads from it seawards along the gully ahead, descend diagonally left to the junction of these tracks. On meeting the tracks turn right, seawards; then, almost immediately, turn left on a path and rise up the next mound. From the top of this mound, look across the dip ahead and note the path nearest the sea: this is your onward route. Descend to the inland side of the dip (keeping right at a fork) and, when you meet a crossing path, turn right towards the sea. In around a minute, where there is a collapsed stone wall on the right, fork left on a faint path rising diagonally along the hillside. Then pick up the path you spotted from the top of the mound — the one nearest the cliff edge — and continue uphill (2h57min). This path contours above the sea, then heads inland through a small fir tree plantation. Once clear of the trees, the masts above Figueira can be seen ahead. Then the path swings back to follow the coast and rises into an open area with good views of the coastline stretching ahead. Soon the ruined fort above Figueira beach comes into view. Eventually the path winds down the cliff to Praia da Figueira *(great care is needed on this steep and stony descent)*. Once at the bottom (3h13min), walk diagonally left, to locate the start of a trail. If the stream here is deep (it's usually just a trickle), head inland to locate stepping stones. Follow this trail (later a track) back to Figueira, where you emerge by the bus stop, just to the left of your starting point.

This circular walk explores some of the wildest country-side in Algarve, out in the far west. A large part of the hike follows the rugged coastline over numerous head-lands, finding quiet sandy bays along the way. While swimmers will be attracted by these bays, the seas here are often rough, with a strong undertow, so choose a calm day. The beaches at Ingrina and Zavial have cafés which may open only at weekends and holidays out of season. This is a hearty, bracing walk. The climbs tend to be short and steep, but frequent. The landscape changes fre-quently, too — with coastal views one moment and wild countryside the next.

Start out from the BUS STOP in **Figueira** by continuing west along the road, with the main part of the village to your right. Ignore a track on the left immediately. *(This is where the Extended walk comes back into Figueira.)* Just after crossing a small BRIDGE (under **5min**), turn left on a narrow road. Ignore a track up left six minutes later. A lone ruined windmill up on the right surveys a rolling countryside chequered with pockets of cultivation. Keep ahead at diagonal track/road crossing (**17min**). *(The return route from Praia das Furnas joins from the left here.)* The road approaches a COMPLEX OF RED-ROOFED BUILDINGS

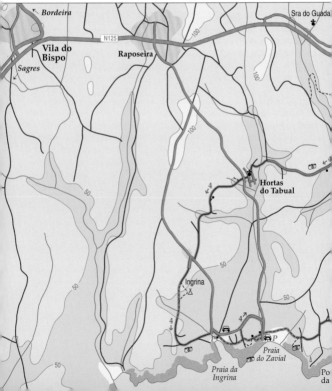

and swings right to skirt round the complex (**20min**), passing the entrance on the left. Rise to reach a crossing track and keep ahead to pass a white house below on the left (**27min**; photograph overeaf). Agaves line the route for a short distance, as the road levels out. In **30min** Hortas do Tabual comes into view ahead. In a landscape of hills and hollows, the road dips and then rises to a junction (**36min**). Skirt the mound ahead by going right, then swing round left, making a U-turn back towards Hortas. In a further four minutes the road reverts to track. Dip right, to cross a stream bed and rise to a T-junction. Turn left towards the village.

Enter **Hortas do Tabual** and turn right at the CROSS-ROADS (**45min**). Almost immediately, turn right again on the main village road. Just before a FOUNTAIN and CHURCH on the right, turn left in front of a WATER TROUGH, onto a track (**46min**). Soon cross the RAPOSEIRA/ZAVIAL ROAD and keep ahead. As the stony track descends into a small valley, ignore a right fork into a field. Then rise up to a track (**55min**), which ends at a house on the left. Turn right along the track, away from the house; then, in a little over a minute, as the track angles to the left, keep ahead on a field track. This faint track undulates beneath a line of

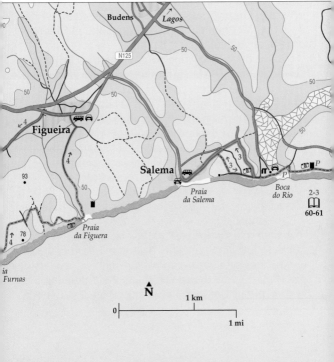

TELEGRAPH POLES which can be seen leading towards a cluster of BUILDINGS — and this is where you are heading. When a track joins from the right (**1h02min**), continue ahead to the RAPOSEIRA/INGRINA ROAD (**1h05min**).

Turn right, cross the road and head seawards down the road to the left, between the buildings opposite (signposted to the INGRINA CAMPSITE). This reverts to a wide track in two minutes. Just over three minutes later, keep ahead on the track to the right of the CAMPSITE ENTRANCE. The track soon becomes a path, which is faint at the outset. Keep heading due south towards the sea, with the campsite over to your left. The track climbing the distant hillside ahead is your ongoing route. Skirt to the right of a clump of EUCALYPTUS TREES (**1h13min**), then pass some screening on the left. Now the path should become obvious again. Reach an open area, maybe with beehives, and cross diagonally left, or head left along a field track, to meet the wide path coming from the campsite (**1h18min**), where you continue to the right. Ignore a track off left (**1h22min**) and start to descend. A minute later, at a T-junction, keep round to the left. There are some magnificent coastal views to enjoy now, as Ingrina comes into full view. At a fork, keep left downhill, to a surfaced ROAD (**1h30min**). Turn left on the road, then either keep ahead to the Ingrina road and turn right, or take a path off right (before a ruin), to cross the **Praia da Ingrina** (Picnic 4b) and reach the cafe three minutes later (**1h33min**).

Leave Praia da Ingrina by crossing the café car park and follow the path along the cliff top. The path dips down to touch a track, then continues up ahead, initially with some concrete posts on the left. Descend to a track (**1h 38min**) and cross straight over* on a path heading towards a house. Below the house, you rejoin the cliff route and come to a junction above Zavial. The path to the left is more difficult, with tree roots underfoot; the one to the right demands a head for heights, but is the easier descent. *Take care when using either route.* You reach **Praia do Zavial** (Picnic 4a) at the right of the café (**1h49min**).

To continue, head seawards across the beach, towards the large rocks at the base of the cliff. Scramble over the rocks to locate the ongoing path at the base of the cliff. Follow this path behind and above the beaches. A stony ascent takes you up to a crossing path (**1h59min**); this is a good picnic spot, with views over Zavial. Turn left and

*There is a cliff-edge path further on, but it is dicey. To avoid the cliff descent to Zavial altogether, turn left on the track, then take the road.

Agaves line the route for a short distance, as the road levels out near a white house (about 27 minutes into the walk).

follow the path up to the right — to a rise where there is a crossing track (**2h03min**) and extensive views back to Sagres and ahead to Ponte da Piedade near Lagos. Go right towards a large CAIRN, but fork left downhill immediately. (The curious might wish to divert right to the cairn, thought to have been a tower at one time.) Keep left as a track joins from the right, but stay ahead as the main track sweeps left inland (**2h06min**). Fork left, then right, to meet a cross-track a few minutes later. Keep right again, to continue in the same direction, on a now quite stony path/track which rounds a shallow gully.

When you come to a wide crossing path, with a small cairn down to the right, at the edge of the cliff (**2h15min**), turn left (north). Soon you will see a white house on a mound ahead and the white mass of Salema along the coast to the right. In just over two minutes, stay with the main path, which forks off right, and head for the mouth of Praia das Furnas cove. When a wall blocks the way, go left. About a minute later, fork right to pass through a gap in the wall. Start into the gradual descent to the cove, and do not be tempted to turn right down any of the many fishermen's paths. Praia das Furnas comes into view, and the path crosses a rocky area, becoming clear again as it continues diagonally towards the beach. Vertigo may be a problem for some on a short stretch where the path traverses close to the cliff edge. Do not cut down to the beach too soon; keep a steady course towards the back of the beach. You reach the **Praia das Furnas** in **2h30min**. *(The Extended walk carries on from this point.)*

To head back inland to Figueira, locate and follow the stony track leading from the back of the beach. This crosses a stream bed to reach a T of tracks. Turn right and cross back over the stream bed to continue. Keep ahead, ignoring a track off right, until you reach the diagonal cross-tracks first encountered at the 17min-point on the outward route (**2h48min**). Turn right here, then turn right again on meeting the surfaced road, back into **Figueira** and the BUS STOP (**3h05min**).

5 FÓIA ROAD • MADRINHA • PÉ DO FRIO • CHILRÃO • FÓIA ROAD

See also photograph page 49

Distance: 11.0km/6.9mi; 2h50min

Grade: moderate-strenuous. There is a descent of 375m/1230ft in the first part which has to be regained on the return. The footpaths and tracks used are generally good underfoot.

Equipment: See pages 44-45.

How to get there and return: 🚗 only accessible by car. From Monchique follow the signs for Fóia. Some 6km from Monchique (200m past the *miradouro*, at the point where the road bends right), park down the second of two tracks close together on the left, in an open area with some ruined buildings.

Shorter walks

1   Fóia road — Madrinha — Fóia road (1.8km/1.1mi; 22min). Easy grade, but rough underfoot in places. Follow the main walk to enjoy the views from the summit of Madrinha. Then return the same way.

2   Fóia road — Pé do Frio — Chilrão — Fóia road (10.3km/6.4mi; 2h42min). Grade and notes as for main walk, but omit the climb to Madrinha.

The *serras* which make up the most northerly part of Algarve are generally dull and monotonous. Their schistose composition generates an acid soil which supports a uniform *matos* consisting mainly of gum cistus, *Cistus ladanifer*. But the Serra de Monchique is altogether different. Its greater height gives it an imposing presence, and its granite composition favours a more varied and interesting flora. This area provides the most demanding walking in Algarve.

After first climbing the nearby summit of Madrinha (803m/2634ft) to enjoy the views, this walk then descends its western slopes, to visit two small villages before circling back by a different route. It starts 200m/yds past the viewpoint near the top of Fóia signposted 'Fonte/Miradouro'. It's not unusual to find one or two locals here, offering to sell home-made produce to passers-by, including honey and *medronho*, a spirit made from the fruit of the strawberry tree (see panel opposite).

Start out at the PARKING PLACE: with your back to the road, go down the track to the right of the small hill. Stay left on the rising track at the fork (under **3min**), and ignore a track off left soon afterwards. Meet a track fork at the top of the rise (**7min**). Now go left uphill to the SUMMIT of **Madrinha** (**11min**), marked by a trig point and a firewatch station. *(Stay right downhill for Shorter walk 2).* This is one of the finest viewpoints in the region and, given a clear day, it is possible to pick out a whole host of landmarks stretching the full breadth of Algarve.

Strawberry tree (Arbutus unedo)

STRAWBERRY TREE

Retrace your steps to the junction of tracks (**15min**). *(Shorter walk 1 retraces the outgoing route from here.)* Turn left and continue down the hill, heading for a cluster of wind turbines. Pass a red and white mast on the right and keep descending on the main track, ignoring any side tracks, with the summit of Picos close by on the left and views to Pé do Frio on the right.

A junction with a ROAD is reached in **50min**. This is the new route to Pé do Frio, but the old route is more scenic, so cross the road and take the track to the right, descending parallel with the road. Stay right at the fork reached two minutes later, to enjoy good views across the valley to Pé do Frio. Where the track swings down left (**54min**), keep ahead on a path, passing a small house up to the right. The field track/path descends, crosses a gully, and bends left. Step round any animal barriers that may be across the field track/path.

AS ITS NAME indicates, you eat only one! The fruits of the strawberry tree are unpalatable, but they make a splendid *aguardente*, a firewater called *medronho*.

The tree flowers in September and October, and it is at this time that the previous year's fruit starts to ripen and really resembles a strawberry. Only then is it ready for collection.

The fruit is fermented in wooden barrels to produce alcohol with only enough water to cover the mass. The natural yeasts already present on the fruit start the fermentation. Mud is used to seal the barrels, with a tube for escaping gases, to protect the alcohol from further oxidation.

By January the fermentation is usually complete, and it is ready for distillation. This process uses a specially-designed copper kettle, which is heated over a wood fire. A medium-sized kettle will handle about 100 kilos of the fermented brew, but the mass needs to be stirred by hand to prevent burning, until it is necessary to fit the tubes ready for distillation. A slow and steady distillation rate gives the best results and produces *medronho* which is about 90% proof. Your visit to Algarve will not be complete without sampling some *medronho* at one of the bars in Caldas...

Rhododendron ponticum, *with the Monchique hills in the background*

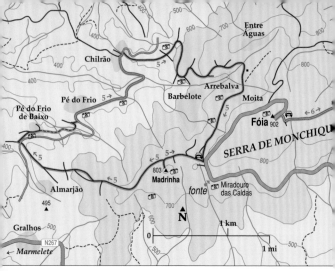

At **1h06min** turn right at the junction, to enter the main part of **Pé do Frio**, the hamlet shown on page 49. Turn left on meeting the road less than a minute later.

Chilrão soon comes into sight. It too is just a scattering of farm houses and has no shops. Keep on the road to pass **Chilrão** (**1h25min**), and stay ahead at the junction two minutes later. Ignore the track joining from the left in **1h32min**, but look for a track ascending to the right less than a minute later (at a point where the road is itself starting to bend away to the right).

Slip into low gear as the uphill section now gets underway, with good views on the left. Stay ahead at the diagonal crossing track (**1h45min**). Seven minutes later, fork right, where a track continues ahead. Stay with the track as the route describes almost a U-turn to the right, back towards Fóia, with a valley on the right. Be sure to keep left in **2h04min**, where a track descends ahead; then, two minutes later, go sharp left, staying with the track. From this sharp bend there are some spectacular views, especially towards the steep terraces just below Madrinha. You can also see a zigzag of tracks below Fóia; this is where our route will eventually take us. Take another sharp turn (**2h09min**), this time to the right, where a track continues ahead. Swing left two minutes later, then keep ahead (**2h21min**).

Terracing brings a neat order and grace to the steep hillsides, as you continue steadily uphill along the main track. As you leave the shade of a EUCALYPTUS WOOD (**2h 23min**), fork right on a woodland track. It becomes clear that you are walking a horseshoe circuit around the valley down to your right. Pé do Frio and Chilrão can both be

72

Caldas de Monchique; the village has recently undergone restoration.

seen below. Soon there is a fork in the track (**2h41min**), where you keep up to the left. All along this section there are fine views down over old terraces and farm clusters. The track rises to join the ROAD (**2h49min**). The PARKING PLACE where the walk began is just to the right (**2h50min**).

6 MONCHIQUE • FÓIA • MONCHIQUE

See map pages 72-73

Distance: 10.6km/6.6mi; 2h20min

Grade: moderate. Monchique is situated at an elevation of around 400m/1300ft, which still leaves 500m/1640ft of climbing before you reach the top of Fóia. Although the route is fairly direct, the going is rarely very steep, which makes the walk less strenuous than it might appear.

Equipment: See pages 44-45.

How to get there: 🚌 by bus from Portimão to Monchique (Timetable 3). Journey time 32-45min. 🚗 by car: park in Monchique's main square or at the viewpoint on the right, as you enter the square.

To return: 🚌 bus back to Portimão (Timetable 3), or 🚗 car

Short walks

1 Monchique — Nossa Senhora de Desterro — Monchique (1.6km/ 1mi; 21min; easy; no special equipment required). Follow the main walk to the ruins of the 17th-century convent; return the same way.

2 Fóia to Monchique (5.6km/3.5mi; 1h20min). Grade as main walk. Take a taxi from Monchique to the top of Fóia (8km) and use the map to walk back down. Start out from the car park, by heading down to the nearest cluster of aerials and dishes, to find the minor surfaced road leading off to the left, signposted to Restaurante Jardim das Oliveiras.

A t 902m/2960ft, Fóia is the highest peak in Algarve, but the summit — adorned as it is with clusters of radio and television masts, a concrete obelisk, restaurant and gift shops — is not especially attractive. However, the views are truly panoramic and, should you be

fortunate to choose a clear day, you can see Sagres on the southern side and out to Cape St Vincent — one of the most westerly tips of mainland Europe; to the north the mountain ranges south of Lisbon are visible. Monchique itself seems to offer little of interest as you arrive in the main square, but you will discover the real character of the place in the narrow streets where the walk begins.

The walk starts at the main square in **Monchique**, the LARGO 5 DE OUTUBRO, where you alight from the bus. Leave the square from the top right-hand corner from where you entered, along the narrow cobbled street to the right called RUA DE PORTO FUNDO. In less than a minute turn left into a narrow alley (TRAVESSA DAS GUERREIRAS) and climb the shallow steps, to cross a narrow street (**2min**) and continue upwards. At the next junction, reached in less than a minute, keep to the right initially, then swing left. Still climbing, swing right in **4min** and continue in a steep ascent out of Monchique. In **6min**, where the road goes down right, keep ahead to join an old trail which leads past a WATER PUMPING STATION and a SHRINE on the wall, both on the left. Good views soon open up back towards Monchique to the left and across to Picota on the right, where you can see the trig point and the fire-watch tower (both visited in Walk 7). Ignore another old trail

The open countryside below Fóia. Some of the flora you can expect to see on this walk in early season are the small funnel-shaped lilac flowers of Romulea bulbocodium, blue Scilla monophyllos — a plant easily distinguished by its single leaf, and the broad-leaved Epipactis helleborine. In Monchique itself, it is interesting to see how bright yellow Bermuda buttercups manage to colonise even the walls of the narrow streets.

which sweeps off to the right (**9min**) and continue ahead to the ruined Franciscan convent dating from 1623, **Nossa Senhora de Desterro** (**11min**). *(Short walk 1 turns back here.)*

Go right as you reach the convent, taking a path which leads directly uphill through the woodland. Cork oaks provide shade as you follow the path which rises to meet an old trail (**13min**). Turn left now to leave the oak woodland and start in a steeper ascent. The trail swings left and rises to pass between crash barriers, onto a surfaced road (**17min**), where you turn left. But be sure to turn right almost immediately, onto a rough track. Just about a minute up this track (**19min**), take the path which leads off to the left. Woodlands shade the way as you climb steadily, to run into a woodland track (**22min**), where you continue to the right uphill.

Scents of pine and eucalyptus mingle as you tread softly on the carpet of forest litter. On meeting the next track (**27min**), on a bend, follow it straight ahead, uphill. Keep steadily uphill, ignoring tracks right and left. When the track bends sharply right (**35min**) there are good open views over to the right. Two minutes later, bend left and continue rising above and around the valley on the left. Ignore a minor track down left and reach a diagonal crossing track (**48min**), just before the track becomes more level. Turn up right here on a very rough track. Fóia comes into view ahead as you rise to meet a road (**50min**), just beyond a bend. Go right along the narrow road towards the summit. There is as much interest in the immediate landscape (photograph pages 74-75) as in the distant views. Terraces woven into steep hillsides suggest a sleep of centuries, isolated farms shimmer in the sun, and the sense of tranquillity is enhanced by the sound of distant cowbells. When you reach the SUMMIT of **Fóia** (**1h12min**), continue to the right, to the shops, restaurant and car parking area.

After taking a break for refreshments, return to **Monchique** the same way (**2h20min**).

7 MONCHIQUE — PICOTA CIRCUIT

See map pages 72-73; see also photograph page 42

Distance: 9.5km/6mi; 2h42min

Grade: moderate. The ascent of 400m/1300ft is mostly gradual and the footpaths and tracks used are mainly good underfoot.

Equipment: See pages 44-45.

How to get there: 🚌 bus from Portimão to Monchique (Timetable 3). Journey time 32-45min.

To return: 🚌 bus from Monchique to Portimão (Timetable 3)

Shorter walk: Monchique — Picota — Monchique (6.6km/4.1mi; 2h; grade as main walk). Start out by walking south from Monchique on the Portimão road for about three minutes, then turn left down a cobbled track, passing a tap on the left. Use the map to climb to Picota, following the main walk in reverse. Return the same way.

Picota is the twin of Fóia, peaking a little lower (at 774m/2540ft). Monchique nestles in the valley between the two. Picota provides interesting walking, with the added bonus of tranquillity on the summit. Botanically it is possibly the more interesting mountain, although the eucalyptus plantations to its north do nothing to help in this respect, since their thirsty roots denature the soil.

Start the walk from the main square in **Monchique**, the Largo 5 de Outubro: head out along the Lisbon road, passing the FISH MARKET and HELIPORT on the right. Take the right fork (**5min**), signposted 'Cruz dos Madeiros', to descend a narrow road. On coming into the hamlet of **Cruz dos Madeiros (7min)**, fork right again, and enjoy the shade of this leafy lane which reverts to track (**8min**). Stay ahead through the cork oak woods, catching glimpses of terraces across the valley to the right. Two minutes after passing tracks off right and left, fork right on a descending path (**13min**), which soon becomes cobbled in parts.

From about the 30min-point in the walk, there are fine views across the valley to Monchique, nestling below the lower slopes of Fóia.

Cross a dirt track two minutes later, to continue down towards the valley floor. Turn left at a junction reached a minute later, along the main trail running parallel with the river below right. When you meet the bend of a road (**18min**), go down right, to cross the river. Almost immediately, as the road rises, fork left into a walled track. The track takes you to a house (**21min**); continue along the right-hand side of the house on the track. Be ready to fork right uphill on a path, to continue alongside a wall. Soon back in a walled-in path, you can enjoy views over this fertile and well-cultivated valley, where orange trees add a splash of colour in winter and spring.

In **25min**, after rising steeply, the path runs into a road and passes a farm on the left. Rise to join a narrow road coming in from the right less than a minute later. Keep right at the fork reached almost immediately and stay with the road to climb back into cork oak woodland. The cork collection point shown on page 42 is passed just before reaching a cross-track (**35min**); turn right here, up an old track, passing a farm on the left. You reach the ALFERCE ROAD just over two minutes later.

Cross directly over the road and, initially, take the narrow path ahead, then the path which heads left uphill towards a stone wall. Continue beside the wall and keep ahead (**40min**). The path soon becomes walled-in as it swings left. Rise onto a road (**42min**) and turn right. In less than a minute, as the road bends left, keep ahead into a path which leads up through terraces. Stay up this path, ignoring a path off left, and rise onto a cross path five minutes later, opposite a water tank. Go left on what becomes track, then roughly surfaced road, through cork oaks. Meet another road less than two minutes later and stay ahead to pass a road left to a farm in a further two minutes. The road now follows along the contour with open views right across the valley to Monchique and Fóia. Rise to pass below a large farm, with silver-coloured silos, up left (**55min**). When you reach another road (**1h01min**), turn left and climb steeply uphill, but watch for a footpath off left through the woods in just over a minute. The young eucalyptus plantation provides some shade as you continue on this path in a steady ascent.

When you again join a road (**1h05min**), turn left. Stay with the road for six minutes, then head right at a fork (**1h11min**). Go right again less than a minute later on a track (initially surfaced with concrete). Keep ahead along the hillside, passing a farm on the left, where the way becomes a rough woodland track. Follow the main track as it wends its way past BUILDINGS and swings left. Keep ahead on the main track in a steady ascent through the eucalyptus. Ignore a track coming from the right (**1h30min**); keep ahead. Very shortly after this junction, reach a high point and crossing tracks (before starting to descend). Look for an ORANGE ARROW/RED DOT: turn right here on a woodland track, which reverts to a path waymarked with ORANGE DOTS.

Turn left as you meet a road (**1h37min**), now heading for the summit, which soon comes into view. The climb is quite steep; clamber over the rocks to reach the TRIG POINT and FIRE-WATCH STATION on **Picota** (**1h47min**). There are fantastic views over towards Fóia and the convent passed in Walk 6. The Barragem da Bravura can be seen in the south, as well as Portimão and Lagos on the coast.

Leave the summit on the far side of the watch-tower from your first approach, following ORANGE DOTS. Descend carefully over the granite rocks, heading for a small saddle and path (roughly 250°; Monchique is over to your right). Soon after joining this path (**1h52min**) look for a woodland track downhill to the right, indicated by yet another ORANGE ARROW on the bedrock; it takes you downhill through a plantation. Ignore minor tracks leaving your route and, when you come to a T-junction, turn right. Keep downhill on meeting a narrow road. When you meet another road on a bend (**2h10min**), turn right to continue downhill. At a T of roads (**2h19min**), turn left.

In just under five minutes you reach the main ALFERCE ROAD, where you again turn left. On approaching the MONCHIQUE/PORTIMÃO ROAD (**2h28min**), turn sharp right to enter a walled-in road, which leads back in the direction from which you have just come, but at a lower level. Just after the road ends three minutes later (past a house), turn left on a track, towards another house. Continue up the path to the left of this house, heading towards Monchique. Just before reaching some apartments, rise onto a cobbled road and go left. As you come to a tap on the right, turn left to the MAIN ROAD (**2h39min**). Turn right here, back to the centre of **Monchique** (**2h42min**).

8 ILHA DO ROSÁRIO CIRCUIT

See map pages 84-85

Distance: 8km/5mi; 1h34min

Grade: easy, mainly level walking along a watercourse *(levada)*

Equipment: See pages 44-45.

How to get there and return: 🚗 only accessible by car. From the Silves roundabout, take the N124 towards Monchique for 4.2km/2.6mi. Turn left at the far end of the Mira-Rio restaurant car park, just after a sharp right bend, and park. Mira-Rio permits parking and using their steps to get to the watercourse. We always buy a drink or snack there as a 'thank you'.

Shorter version of the main walk (6.4km/4mi; 1h12min). Park in the lay-by on the left, 3.9km/2.4mi from Silves roundabout, just before the road bends sharp right. Take the roughly-surfaced narrow road down left, just beyond the lay-by. In under a minute, you will reach the point where the road crosses the watercourse. Turn left on the path alongside this *levada* and pick up the main walk from the 11min-point. Leave the walk at the same point on your return.

Bounded by two rivers, and a haven of peace and solitude, Rosário might as well be an island — as its name 'Ilha' suggests. This delightful bucolic walk follows a watercourse *(levada)* around the hillside, trapped between cliffs and the river, then completes the circuit of the hill by quiet country lanes. One of the pleasures of this walk is the ease by which you escape to landscapes quite unlike any others in Algarve. Since this walk is handily situated close to Silves, you could try Walk 9 in the morning, have lunch in Silves, explore the town, and then enjoy this stroll.

Start the walk by descending the steps to the left of the MIRA-RIO RESTAURANT to the *levada* below. Cross the watercourse and turn left along the adjacent footpath. At this point the **Ribeira de Odelouca** is quite close on the right, and the path passes housing on the left. Orange groves are a feature as the *levada* contours the hillside. The watercourse crosses a field track in **8min** (a more direct return route, emerging near the Mira-Rio restaurant) and a roughly-surfaced narrow road less than four minutes later (**11min**). *(The Shorter version joins here.)* The road remains alongside the *levada* for a while, and you soon cross it again. A small PUMPING STATION on the left marks the **16min**-point; the return route rejoins the *levada* here. The elevated path gives good views over the river, a peaceful setting where you may see some birds. After **24min**, cross left over the *levada*, to continue along the other side, then cross back again less than two minutes later. At this point make a diversion onto a rocky promontory which sits at the CONFLUENCE of the **Odelouca**

The levada *(watercourse) and the Ribeira de Odelouca; below: at the confluence of the Odelouca and Arade rivers*

and **Arade** rivers. This is a favourite haunt of the local fishermen, a great viewpoint and ideal picnic stop.

Back on the *levada*, as you approach the narrow surfaced road crossed earlier (**31min**; by a house on the right), the path crosses back to the left-hand side of the watercourse. Around two minutes later, you enjoy views back to the river confluence. Then Silves comes into view ahead (**42min**). As the *levada* swings away from the river, you might like to take a path downhill to a riverside café/bar (only open in high season). Otherwise, keep ahead as the *levada* runs underground for a short stretch. Cross a track leading up left

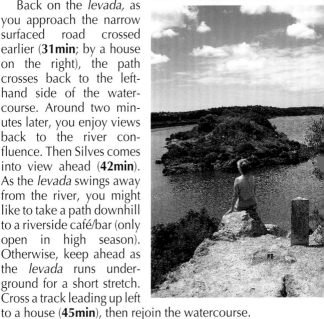

to a house (**45min**), then rejoin the watercourse.

When you reach a HAMLET and crossing track (**49min**), leave the *levada* path and turn right along the track, which immediately crosses over the *levada*. The track now traverses more open, cultivated countryside, while the watercourse, initially up to the left, crosses overhead four minutes later, running towards Silves. Keep left at a junction (**58min**), to pass the CLINICA DO FALACHO on the left. Ignore tracks from the left and right. Now on road, ascend through the hamlet of **Vale da Lama** (**1h13min**), from where there are fine views over the surrounding countryside. Descend to another road (**1h18min**), turn left, to pass the small PUMPING STATION on the right. This was the 16min-point in the walk: cross the small bridge over the *levada* and turn right, to return to your PARKING PLACE (**1h34in**).

81

9 SILVES CIRCUIT

See also photograph page 24 **Distance**: 7.5km/4.7mi; 1h46min

Grade: easy. Little climbing is involved, and the tracks and paths used are mostly good underfoot.

Equipment: See pages 44-45.

How to get there and return: 🚌 by bus from Portimão or Albufeira to Silves (Timetables 4, 5). Journey time 35-42min. 🚂 by train to Silves station (Timetable 9); the station lies some 2km/1.25mi south of Silves, but there are bus connections to the town. 🚗 by car: Park by the ring road, in the large parking areas provided on the south side of Silves.

Short walk: Silves — windmill — Silves (4.8km/3mi; 1h05min). Follow the main walk for 32 minutes; return the same way.

Silves is a lovely old town situated on the River Arade. Apart from enjoying the ambience of the town square, there are several places of particular interest — including the castle, the cathedral, the museum and the old port area. Legend has it that Silves (or Cylpes, Chelb or Cilves, to use earlier names), was founded on its present site by the Cynetes some one thousand years BC, and since that time it has been occupied by a succession of races from all over Europe and Africa — including the Greeks and later the Romans, around the first century AD. Its subsequent history is turbulent, with bloody battles, times of peace and prosperity, total decline, and devastation by earthquakes. The museum is worth a visit, to see the coins and ceramics and other relics of these past civilisations and events. It is uphill to the right of the tower of the main gateway, in the old Moorish city walls, off the main square.

Windmill above Silves (Picnic 9)

If you park in the car park or arrive by train, follow the signs for 'Câmara' (Town Hall), to direct you up to the main square. **Start the walk** at the MAIN SQUARE in **Silves**: walk through the high arched gateway of the TOWER and head uphill, passing to the left of the CATHEDRAL (Sé; **3min**). The walk continues to the right at the junction just past the cathedral. (But first cross the junction and then go right to visit the castle, before returning to this point to continue; it is open daily except holidays from 09.00-19.00 in summer, but closes a little earlier in winter.) At the next junction, a minute later, keep left downhill, staying beneath the walls of the CASTLE on the left. Coming to a crossroads (**9min**), turn left and then immediately fork right, on a track which leads between a fenced-off orange grove and large car park. Looking back, there are some especially fine views of Silves castle to be enjoyed.

As you approach a smallholding (**16min**), the track becomes concreted and continues up to the WATERCOURSE followed in Walk 8. Cross the narrow concrete footbridge and turn right on the path alongside the *levada*. In **17min** the path leads uphill to the left, towards a group of houses. As you reach them,

I T WAS THE ARABS who left behind the most impressive remains to be seen in Silves — the castle, the Albarranian Towers, the Alma-dinna walls, and the underground well. The castle enjoyed its heyday under the Moors in the 10th-12th centuries. During that period Silves was an important city, more important even than Lisbon. Situated in a rich agricultural region, it boasted opulent buildings, a thriving port, and markets.

The decline began in 1189, when Silves came under siege as part of the third crusade to oust the infidels from Algarve and spread Christianity. The slow decline of the city was finally completed by the earthquake of 1755, when the castle, the tower, and the town hall were badly damaged, and Silves ceased to be the capital of Algarve. Many of the walls are still intact, as is the underground well — romantically named 'Cisterna da Moura Encantada' (the enchanted Moorish girl's well).

You can enjoy all this at your leisure. If you look northeast as you walk the castle walls, you can see the old windmill shown opposite, perched on a hilltop. This lies on our route and is the destination of the Short walk. The cathedral, which you pass on the way to the castle, was built in Gothic style by King Afonso X during the last part of the 13th century. It became the cathedral of Algarve until, in the middle of the 16th century, the seat of the bishop was removed to Faro. Little is known about the fate of the silver treasures or the large library which were believed to have existed.

less than two minutes later, turn left on the narrow surfaced road; soon, at the next road junction, turn sharp right. Now you are heading towards the windmill, which is clearly in sight. At the road reached in **21min**, bend left, then continue around to the right, heading momentarily back towards Silves and the towering arches of the aqueduct. At the junction of roads by the AQUEDUCT (**24min**), turn sharp left. Keep right at the fork encountered almost immediately. Turn right off the main road onto a lesser road (**28min**), to keep the windmill now up to the left. About a minute up the road, turn left on a track which dips towards the windmill then sweeps right towards a pink house. Pass the front of the house, then go left, straight up to the WINDMILL (Picnic 9; **33min**). There is a superb panorama over rolling *matos*-covered hills, with cultivated valleys and an excellent view of Silves. Portimão is visible on the seaward side, and the hills of the Serra de Monchique to the north. Close at hand, sticky-leaved cistus, *Cistus ladanifer*, and lavender, *Lavandula stoechas,* dominate in the dense vegetation; the green-winged orchid, *Orchis morio*, also finds a foothold.

Leave the windmill to continue along the undulating ridge, with your back to the sea. Follow the path along the ridge, keeping to the central spine. Good views open up now towards the Bastos Valley ahead on the right. Follow the path to the end of the ridge (**42min**), then turn left downhill, alongside a fenced enclosure. You pass a farmhouse on the left. At the end of the descent, turn right on a rising track, to meet a T-junction (**45min**). Go left, then keep round to the right at the top of the rise. Turn right almost immediately, along a track which at first keeps above the wooded valley down to the left. It then descends to a crossing of tracks (**52min**), where you turn sharp left to continue downhill. Keep on this main track, which heads south beside a stream bed. Masses of lavender, olives and carobs now join the eucalyptus as you wind down through the valley. On joining a wide stabilised track (**1h08min**), turn left.

This track leads away from the *matos*-covered hills and back through cultivation towards Silves. The track

Fábrica do Inglês — a cultural centre in Silves, incorporating the cork museum

becomes surfaced road (**1h14min**) as you approach the outskirts of the town, where you keep to the right-hand road on meeting housing. Turn left into a narrow walkway (**1h16min**, just before a huge palm), and climb up steps which curve around to the right. A surfaced road is met one minute later. Turn left and, in under two minutes, take a track up right to the *levada*. Cross the lock gate and turn left. Follow the path alongside the watercourse, which is now on your left. Cross a surfaced road (**1h27min**; there is a restaurant just off to the right here, closed Wednesdays) and continue alongside the *levada*. The circuit is complete when you reach the concrete FOOTBRIDGE (**1h31min**) crossed earlier in the walk; here turn down the track on the right to retrace your steps back to **Silves** (**1h46min**).

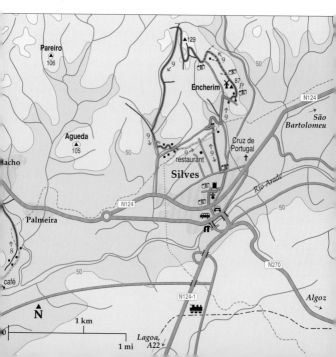

10 BENAGIL • MARINHA • ALBANDEIRA • SENHORA DA ROCHA • BENAGIL

See also photograph page 10

Distance: 10.8km/6.7mi; 2h40min

Grade: moderate. There is a steep valley, difficult to cross, in the final section of the walk.

Equipment: See pages 44-45.

How to get there and return: (Timetable 10) or to Benagil. The approach road to Benagil is located on the N125, 3km east of the Lagoa roundabout and opposite the International School. It is signposted from the Lagoa approach only, but signs appear at later junctions along this 5km stretch. Park near the café/restaurant 'O Litoral' at the top of the hill, before descending to Benagil bay. *Note:* This walk is easily followed in reverse from Senhora da Rocha. Either take a taxi from Armacão de Pêra or walk the 2.5km/1.6mi from Hotel Garbe in Armacão, initially towards Porches, then turn left opposite the Cepsa Garage.

Short walks: Both are easy.

1 Benagil — Praia da Marinha — Benagil (4.8km/3mi; 1h). Follow the main walk to the beautiful beach at Marinha. Return the same way.

2 Benagil — Praia de Albandeira — Benagil (8.0km/5mi; 1h40min). Follow the main walk to Praia de Albandeira, a small inlet, where there are café facilities in season. Return the same way.

This is another very picturesque section of the coast which is full of interest — from wild flowers to spectacular beaches. In our view, the beach at Marinha rates as one of the loveliest in Algarve and will probably stay so as long as it remains remote and difficult to get to. It lies in a beautiful natural setting and has the benefit of a small café/bar which is open only in season. The coastline along this section is extremely photogenic (see page 10 and overleaf), so be sure to carry plenty of film.

Benagil, where the walk starts, is a small fishing village where, if you wander down to the seafront, you will see the colourful fishing boats which are so typically Algarvian. Fish is still an important part of the diet in Portugal, and it figures prominently on the menu in cafés and restaurants. Sardines *(sardinhas)* are a speciality of the

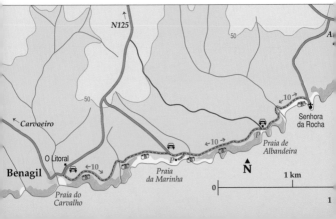

area and, freshly caught and grilled (photograph page 15), they bear no relationship to the more familiar tinned product. They are at their best in the summer season and, traditionally, they are served with boiled potatoes. The finest accompaniment is a chilled bottle of *vinho verde*. The other national fish dish, which is even more popular, is *bacalhau*, dried salted cod. Cod used to be caught by Portuguese fishermen along the Grand Banks off Newfoundland, but now it mainly comes from Norway. The catch is salted, sun-dried and sold as flat, cardboard-like pieces which you'll see and smell in the supermarkets and markets all over Portugal. *Bacalhau*, pronounced 'backle-yow', is desalted and reconstituted by soaking in water and then can be cooked by any one of many hundreds of recipes. In a restaurant which caters primarily for locals there may be several *bacalhau* dishes on offer. Well-prepared and cooked in a tasty sauce, it is really delicious … but if you try it when it is not at its best, then the chances are that it will be your last try!

Start the walk from the CAFÉ O LITORAL at the top of the hill at **Benagil**: head down towards the bay. Turn left to mount the steps immediately before a RESTAURANT (**1min**), and notice how the upper steps are cut out of the rock face. Continue along the path, keeping right at the fork, to head towards the coast. From here onwards it becomes a coastal path leading away from Benagil. There is a wealth of wild flowers along this stretch in spring, including the tassel hyacinth, *Muscari comosum*, the woodcock orchid, *Ophrys scolopax* (which is not so common elsewhere in the region), the yellow bee orchid, *Ophrys lutea*, and many of the species already mentioned on page 59. Coastline erosion provides some interesting bays and weird formations too, which become especially photogenic later in the walk.

In **14min** the path starts to lead inland, to cross an inlet two minutes later. But first there is a diagonal descent to the left, before you go down right to cross the inlet and scramble up the far side, where you find the continuation of the coastal path (**20min**). Now you are at a wonderfully scenic part of the coast, and the views along the cliff, taking in all the incredible rock formations, are quite fantastic. Ahead is the CAR PARK for Marinha (with picnic tables; **26min**).

Cross the car park to descend the steps in the far corner and continue along the surfaced path which is stepped in places. If you are stopping for a swim or just for photographs or refreshments, turn right down the steps three minutes later, to the superb sandy beach — **Praia da Marinha** (Picnic 10a). Otherwise continue along the path which leads back to the cliff top and continues as the coastal path. As you approach a fence (**32min**), pass a large open sea-worn blowhole, and stay with the path as it skirts the fenced area on the seaward side. Coastal views along this walk include some tantalising sandy beaches which seem only to be accessible by boat. The one seen from here is shown on page 10. An inlet is encountered shortly (**36min**): walk down diagonally left to cross it and, as you rise into a clearing five minutes later, take the rough track which leads you back to the cliff edge. The rugged coastline, layered in strata of gold and cream, and sculptured into intriguing shapes by the restless energy of the sea, presents endless patterns. Another, shallow inlet is reached in **44min**. Here the naked man orchid, *Orchis italica*, finds a home amongst the rich flora. Then you come to the larger inlet of **Praia de Albandeira** (Picnic 10b; **48min**).

Continue behind the café/bar: cross the footbridge behind the café and continue along the coastal path. There are views ahead of Armação de Pêra, which looks

like villa-land from this distance (but you will turn back before it is reached). At **55min** a deep inlet requires an inland detour; then head back to the coast, and watch out for more blow-holes. In **1h02min** a very deep inlet is encountered: this one is only negotiable by footpaths which are difficult in places. Set off inland, staying at a high level, and ignore the first strong path descending to the right soon encountered. Go down, diagonally right, following the *second* strong path (it is marked with RED DOTS, but they are not easily seen from this direction). This is a steep and awkward descent towards the back of the beach. Reach the bottom in **1h09min** and turn left towards the back of the inlet, to find a path which goes uphill to a track on the far side of the inlet. Waymarked turns —right, left, right — lead you to a path which continues above this track, back in the direction of the sea. The superb beach at **Senhora da Rocha** is fully in view from a small headland (**1h 15min**), and you pass the steps leading to the beach two minutes later.

Continue past the steps, if you want to visit the Romanesque chapel of Nossa Senhora da Rocha on the headland (turn right at the junction reached in **1h19min**). Some cafés and restaurants lie to the left of this junction, and Armação de Pêra is 2 km further east. But our walk ends at this junction, from where we retrace our steps to **Benagil** (**2h40min**).

The simple white church of Nossa Senhora da Rocha (Our Lady of the Rock) sits on a bluff dividing two coves. Although it was built in the 17th century, the two Visigothic columns used in its construction suggest that an earlier temple may well have existed on this site. Weekends see the local fishermen making their way to this headland. Taking up positions on the very edge, they are able to cast their lines out to sea.

11 CERRO — CONQUEIROS — PICO ALTO CIRCUIT

See map pages 96-97   **Distance**: 10km/6.2mi; 2h25min

Grade: moderate. The trig point on Pico Alto stands at an elevation of 276m/905ft; Cerro itself lies on almost the same contour. There are two uphill sections: the climb up to the trig point is short and steep, while the later climb is more gradual. *Note:* The main walk route outlined below is the most interesting, but can be overgrown. We carry secateurs to cut back rogue brambles and smile cheerily at the local who always pops up to tell us the route is no longer viable. Here are two alternative starts, if you don't want to get scratched. 1) Stay ahead two minutes along. At the T-junction, turn left downhill. You rejoin the main walk in 7min, at the 17min-point in the main walk. 2) Head along the ridge road towards Pico Alto. In around 10min, just after passing an old well and water tank down right and *before* a track forking left by a bus stop, turn right down a track signposted to two *casas* (houses). As the track ends, follow a path to the right, pass a ruin on the left, and join a path forking left downhill (the 12min-point in the main walk).

Equipment: See pages 44-45.

How to get there and return: 🚗 only accessible by car. Cerro lies 3.6km northwest of Alte. Approaching on the N124, turn north into Alte on the more westerly of the two entry roads, and turn left almost immediately, following the sign to Santa Margarida. Turn left again in the centre of Santa Margarida. Park 1.8km further on, beyond the dip with a high white wall on the left. The walk starts on the road to the right, in the dip.

Shorter version of the main walk (9km/5.6mi; 2h12min). Moderate, but with only one uphill section. Follow the main walk to the 1h39min-point, then keep ahead. Walk along the road towards Cerro for 1km, then fork left on a walled-in trail just before the Loulé boundary sign (or stay on the road). Pick up the main walk again just after the 1h59min-point.

Short walks

1   Cerro — Pico Alto village — Cerro (5.6.km/3.5mi; 1h16min; easy-moderate). Follow the main walk to the 12min-point and keep ahead along the trail, using the map to navigate to the road along the top of the ridge. Turn right here; in 1km you will reach Pico Alto village. Follow the road round a bend to the left, then turn left down an old trail. Pick up the main walk just after the 1h39min-point, to walk back to Cerro.

2   Cerro — Pico Alto — Cerro (7.6km/4.7mi; 1h48min; easy). Follow Short walk 1 to Pico Alto, but keep ahead into the village where the track/road goes left. Then use the map to reach the trig point on Pico Alto. The path (waymarked in blue) leaves from between the first and second houses on the right, *before* a palm tree. Return the same way.

Cerro, Conqueiros and Pico Alto, like the villages of Alte and Pena, lie in the Barrocal region of Algarve. The Barrocal is a lens-shaped area of limestone which stretches from Cape St Vincent in the west, reaching its widest around the centre of Algarve (about 20km/12.5mi wide), before tapering out somewhere near Tavira. The limestones are dolomites and marls which are seen as whitish rocks, often weathering to dull grey. These are best observed in the scrub-covered ridges which form

View north (inland) from the summit of Pico Alto, to Messines and the hills of the Serra de Monchique.

crests running parallel with the coast, as here on Pico Alto or, better still, in Walk 15 (Rocha da Pena; photograph page 105). The rich red soil *(terra rossa)* in the valleys between the ridges is highly fertile, and it is these areas which form the garden of Algarve. Orchards abound, and the crops include orange, fig, almond and carob. The almonds are at their most spectacular in January and February when their delicate white and pale pink flowers are sprinkled randomly across the valleys and it is easy to see why they are sometimes called 'Algarvian snow.'

The plants give a good clue to the various distinct geological regions of Algarve, and the Barrocal provides the richest and most interesting flora. Many flowers typical of the region are seen on this walk, including wild jasmine, *Jasminum fruticans*, orchids, and the striking *Scilla peruviana*. Even the scrub *(matos)* is characteristic; there are more details of this in Walk 15. This walk leads through some timeless hamlets and a landscape created by generations of farmers living off the land.

Start the walk in the dip with the TALL WHITE WALL: head down the road towards Cerro village. Pass a WASHHOUSE on the left and, in less than two minutes, turn left on a track with a WATER STORAGE AREA on the left corner. Wind through the old hamlet of **Cerro** and, as the track ends, go diagonally right and then left, to continue in the same direction. Here, give a cheery greeting to a helpful local who may warn you that the way is overgrown. In spring, weeds may obscure the start of the path, but it soon becomes clear that you are on an old trail (secateurs could help at the start, see 'Grade', opposite). Where vegetation blocks the trail, continue alongside, down to the right.

The hamlet of Conqueiros soon comes into view ahead on the valley floor. In **12min** turn sharp right down a path, into the valley below. The path soon becomes a rough field track, before meeting the CERRO/CONQUEIROS ROAD (opposite a small farmhouse; **17min**). Turn left down this road (right leads to Cerro). A peaceful rural ambience pervades this valley planted with olives, carobs and oranges; the heady scent of orange blossom filling the air in season. Just before reaching the hamlet, note the old WELL down to the right, on the far side of a wall (**25min**). Then rise up to walk through **Conqueiros** (**28min**). Continue ahead as the road reverts to track, ignoring strong tracks right and left. The giant reed, *Arundo donax*, marks a stream bed down to the left.

Ignore a track forking right uphill to a farm, pass beneath a high cork oak arching over the track, then fork left on a path, to cross a small stream bed (**48min**). The path rises, passes to the left of a farm building, and meets a crossing track less than two minutes later. Cross over and keep ahead on a field track, which reverts to path. Stay with the track/path as it skirts to the left of a citrus grove and then a field, heading towards the Pico Alto ridge. The path gradually heads towards a fence with concrete posts, over to the right. Cross the overflow stream flowing from a WATER TANK on the right (**53min**). Less than a minute later, the path heads across the top end of the fence and continues between a terrace on the right and a bank on the left. After dipping across an eroded channel, the path rises through a patch of cistus. When you meet a faint diagonal crossing track (**57min**), keep ahead on the main path, making for a clump of trees (which obscure a ruined farmhouse ahead). The path continues up the bank by the trees and emerges to pass to the left of the ruin. Turn right across the top edge of the ruin into an ALMOND GROVE (**1h**). Head left through the grove, then go right on a track, to continue contouring along the ridge with wide-reaching views.

At a junction of tracks (**1h08min**), when the motorway viaduct comes into view ahead, turn left uphill. (But you could turn right downhill here for seven minutes, to a road where there is an excellent café/restaurant just to the right; closed Tuesdays.) Get into low gear for a short steep climb to the SUMMIT of **Pico Alto** (**1h20min**). This is the spot for a picnic, with fantastic views over much of the surrounding countryside. And around your feet there are yet more orchids, one of particular interest being the mirror orchid — or rather a special form of it, in which the lip of the flower has become elongated to resemble an insect. It is *Ophrys speculum ssp lusitanica*.

To continue, return to where the uphill track comes in from the right. Take the path to the left here, pass through the wall, then head right along the centre of the ridge. Ignore a strong path forking off right. You emerge in a field with a large tree in the centre (**1h27min**). The path heads across the field, to the right of this tree, to a rise from where the Pico Alto trig point is visible behind you. Stay on the path as it continues along the left-hand side of the ridge. On coming to a junction of paths (**1h34min**), turn right through a gap in a wall. Then skirt to the left of a bush and follow a strong path across the middle of the ridge.

Soon you enter a walled-in trail. You reach the centre of **Pico Alto** VILLAGE less than five minutes later, emerging between two houses, with a palm tree to the right. Turn left here. Reach the road on a bend (**1h39min**) and turn right. *(Short walks 1 and 2 come in on this bend.)* In under a minute, turn left to descend an old trail. Ignore a trail up right by an enclosed WATER TANK, two minutes later, and keep ahead. This pleasant elevated trail affords good views over the valley to the south, towards the Messines ridge. Stay ahead as a track joins from the right, but turn down right when you meet a cross-track (**1h45min**). The track soon reverts to path. Ignore a fork down right but, when the path forks (**1h46min**), go left, to continue contouring. Just over three minutes later, reach a cross-track and turn left uphill. At a T-junction less than three minutes later, with a WATER TANK down right, turn left uphill. Stay on this track, which rises at first, then levels out and passes behind a building on the right. Keep ahead into a walled track which swings left to reach the ROAD (**1h59min**).

Cross the road and go right immediately, on an old trail. Pass a ruin on the left and ignore a fork to the left. Keep ahead as a short track enters from the road on the right (at the LOULÉ BOUNDARY; **2h01min**). The trail moves away from the road towards a ruined farm complex (**Cumeada**), where the onward trail is overgrown. Go left to wind through the complex. Then skirt to the left of a huge carob tree (**2h03min**) and pick up a faint path to the left of a raised THRESHING FLOOR. Head diagonally right across a field. When you rejoin the trail, turn left. Two minutes later, at a white building, go right and then left, to pass the front of this row of renovated houses. The trail becomes a track at this point, and soon swings right, back to the road: keep ahead along another trail here. Just after a ruin on the left you reach the earthen trail forking down left (**2h10min**). This was the 12min-point in the walk: stay ahead to return to your CAR (**2h25min**).

Distance: 13.0km/8.1mi; 3h

Grade: moderate. There is a climb to the trig point of Rocha dos Soidos at 467m/1530ft, but it is long and steady rather than steep. Some of the paths and tracks used in the walk are very stony underfoot. If gates are encountered from the 1h06min-point, they are open to allow access. At time of writing, however, they were not being used.

Equipment: See pages 44-45.

How to get there and return: 🚗 only accessible by car. See Car tour 3, page 31, for details of how to get there and where to park.

Shorter walk: Alte circuit (10.8km/6.7mi; 2h27min; moderate). Complete the main walk, but miss out the diversion to the trig point by continuing straight ahead at the junction (1h20min), following the notes from the 1h53min-point.

Short walk: Alte — first lime kiln — Alte (4.6km/2.9mi; 1h01min; easy). Follow the main walk for 31 minutes, then return to Alte a different way, by using the notes for the end of the walk (from the 2h30min-point).

This circular walk explores the country to the east and north of Alte. It offers an interesting mix of scenery and contrasts, passing through the natural prickly vegetation typical of the limestone region of Algarve into more pastoral regions of cultivation. Lime kilns dot the way in the first section of the walk. These round structures were once used to burn limestone which produced lime used for building and to whitewash houses.

Start the walk in the centre of **Alte**: walk to the right of the CHURCH, following the 'FONTE' signs. On reaching the fountain area (*fonte;* **6min**), continue on the narrow surfaced road to the left, alongside the RIVER (Picnic 12). The main picnic area, with WC, is reached in **12min**.

When the surfaced road runs out, continue ahead to join a track. Carob trees afford some shade beside the river, its banks splashed pink with oleander. (Note the path descending to the left in **16min**; this is your return route.)

In around **21min**, immediately after a stone wall topped with concrete posts on the left, turn left into a field track. Stay right as the track forks left, to follow an old trail enclosed by stone walls (the trail *does* continue ahead, despite invasive vegetation). Head up through groves of olive and carob trees. Watch out in early spring for the charming yellow jonquil, *Narcissus gaditanus*, which is so miniature that you could easily miss it. The trail reduces to a path just before meeting a cross-path in **30min**, where you turn right. (Left is your return route.) Pass an old LIME KILN on the left (**31min**), the first of several you will encounter. *(The Short walk turns back here.)* A minute later, ignore a path up left (you will descend this path on your return).

Cultivation is left behind now as you head into the *matos,* where the warm air is scented with the perfume of rosemary, *Rosmarinus officinalis*, very abundant in this area. The route is now taking you in a very gradual ascent along a red earthen path, slightly to the right of the densely-vegetated shallow valley floor. Follow the line of the valley, passing more lime kilns. You emerge from the valley at a tourists' hunting area, where the path becomes a track. Just keep heading in the same direction, winding down into the valley ahead and catching views of Rocha da Pena (Walk 15). Eventually the route swings left and descends more steeply through the *matos.*

At the bottom of the descent, turn sharp left on another track (**1h06min**), and head up a small valley. Rocha da Pena is now behind you. The track, now fenced on the left, rises to a junction (**1h15min**); keep ahead here, circling to the left of a small bowl of hills at the head of the valley.

The track rises to a junction (**1h20min**), where you take the right-hand fork to start the climb to the trig point on Rocha dos Soidos.

Apart from the waterfalls just below Alte, its main attraction is this spring, Fonte Pequena, and another spring half a kilometre further along the river — Fonte Grande, with a well-equipped picnic site, café, bar/restaurant and car parking (Car tour 3, Picnic 12).

(But go straight on for the Shorter walk.) Stay with the main track as it winds up the hill. Panoramic views open up as you start to rise, with Rocha da Pena over to the right. Around the **1h32min**-point, just before reaching a walled-in track ahead, turn right on a small path which climbs to the trig point. (At the start of this path there is a wall to the left and a small concrete building to the right.) From the TRIG POINT on **Rocha dos Soidos** (**1h37min**) there are superb views all around. Across the valley, to the north, the village of Sarnadas can be seen and, beyond it, a patchwork of cultivation rolling away into the distance.

Return from the trig point by the same route, until you reach the start of the trig point diversion (**1h53min**); here turn right to continue. Before the fence on the left turns up right and blocks the way ahead, go through the gate on the left (agile walkers now use stones to step over the fence ahead) and continue in the same direction, to rejoin the onward stony trail. It leads back towards Alte, staying level for a time, and overlooking the shallow valley of the outward route. After the trail becomes a track and swings right on approaching a house at **Soidos de Baixo** (**2h12min**), go left down a field track. Follow it towards a small brick building, but continue downhill (with the

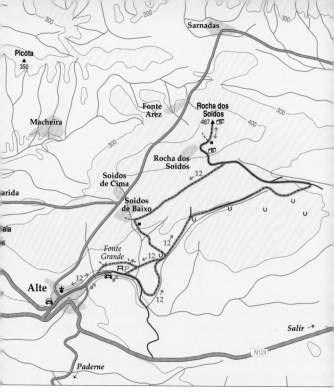

building over to the left) before it is reached. The rough track keeps descending until it reaches a crossing path (**2h17min**). Turn left and skirt above a field, which is below to the right. Stay on the path, which bends right between two fields. The strong path then descends through the *matos* to the bottom of the valley, where it meets the original outward trail (**2h29min**).

Turn right and pass the first lime kiln encountered on the walk (**2h30min**; *the Short walk rejoins here*). At the fork a minute later, keep right, leaving your outward route, to return to Alte a different way. There is a wall on the left of this stony path. Continue to the left (**2h35min**), and stay ahead where a path goes up right*, to enter a wooded area. The path descends gradually at first, but then more steeply. It is rather difficult underfoot before you join the main track (**2h40min**). A right turn here leads back to Alte; you pass the main picnic site just four minutes later. Follow your outgoing route back to **Alte** (**3h**).

*Or take the path to the right, then soon fork left, along the top of the valley down to the left. In four minutes step right through a low wall and continue in the same direction. Stay left at cross-paths, then drop left down the terrace wall and descend gradually along the hillside. When you reach a road, go right, back to the 9min-point in the walk.

13 PADERNE • CASTELO • AZENHAL • PADERNE

Distance: 14km/8.7mi; 3h05min

Grade: easy-moderate. Some footpaths, but the walk is mainly on tracks — sometimes stony, but mostly good underfoot; uphill sections are few.

Equipment: See pages 44-45.

How to get there: 🚌 by bus from Albufeira to Paderne (Timetable 7). Journey time 21min. 🚗 by car: park near the stadium and health centre. *To return*: 🚌 bus from Paderne to Albufeira (Timetable 7), or 🚗 car

Short walks: All of these varied and interesting versions are easy.

1 Paderne — Castelo — Paderne (6.9km/4.3mi; 1h20min). Follow the main walk as far as the castle and return to the motorway, then pick up the main walk again at the 2h29min-point.

2 Paderne — Castelo — Albufeira road (7.2km/4.5mi; 1h35min). Follow the main walk to the 1h33min-point, then turn left to the road, for a bus to Albufeira.

3 Paderne — old bridge — Paderne (8.0km/5mi; 1h42min). Follow the main walk to the castle and on to the bridge (51min). Return from the bridge, following the main walk from the 2h14min-point.

4 Paderne circuit (9.4km/5.8mi; 1h45min). This walk includes the castle, bridge, and watermill. Follow the main walk to the 51min-point. Turn right (instead of left) just over the bridge, and follow the footpath along the river to the mill. Cross the weir to the far bank and follow the track back to the motorway bridge (see footnote on page 101). Return by picking up the main walk at the 2h29min-point.

Alternative walk: Paderne — Azenhal — Paderne (11.5km/7.1mi; 2h 34min). Follow the main walk to the 1h12min-point, then keep right, downhill, on the track. After three minutes (1h15min)*, follow the main track off right (towards the castle). The track passes a ruined farm building, becoming a field track along the ridge top as it heads northeast. Follow it round to the left, beneath electricity cables and to the left of a pylon.** As the track swings right, keep ahead on a path towards the motorway and a white farmhouse. The faint path leads down into a field. Head across the field for only 25 paces, keeping to the right, and then turn right through a gap in the foliage. Beyond the gap go diagonally left; then, almost at once, swing back left towards the white farmhouse. A wall on your left and another wall ahead funnel you into an old path descending into the valley. On meeting an old trail in the bottom, turn right. Keep right at the fork a minute later and right again at the next fork. You emerge on the river bank (1h30min). To the left is Azenhal; to the right is your continuation: pick up the main walk at the 2h01min-point.

*Option 1, marked * → on the map:* At the 1h15min-point stay ahead on the track. In the dip below the motorway, go right on a path, with an overgrown old trail on the left. In a further 3min, go left, then right to join the old trail. (The track rising towards the motorway at this point leads to the motorway access road mentioned below, then to the 1h56min-point in the main walk.) Take the path to the left at the fork a minute later, and rise diagonally right, to meet a tarmac motorway access road (1h30min). Turn right here, then turn right again.

**Option 2, marked ** → on the map, very steep:* Stay right with the field track into a field. Keep to the left of the field, and go left through the gap at the bottom of the field. Head right to the next pylon (fine views). *Carefully* descend the steep path from here to the river, emerging close by Azenhal and the main route to the left.

Paderne Castle (Picnic 13), from the bridge over the Quarteira River

Paderne Castle dates back to the times of the Moors. Built on a hill and surrounded on three sides by the River Quarteira, it had a role in the defence of the region during the period of Arab occupation.

Start the walk from **Paderne** STADIUM on the BOLIQUEIME ROAD below the town. Head towards Purgatório, passing a CEMETERY on the left. Then ignore a first turn-off left (the return route) but take the *second* left (**3min**), signed 'FONTE/CASTELO'. Follow this lane through cultivation, to pass a fountain (*fonte;* **14min**). Very soon, at a fork, bear right on a track. The castle now comes into view ahead, beyond orange and olive groves. Stay on the main track, passing under the MOTOR-WAY. At a fork (**30min**), where the main track curves left up to the castle, keep ahead towards the river on a minor track. Almost immediately, take the diagonal path climbing steeply left up the hillside. In spring, look out for orchids on this climb, including the lovely *Ophrys bombyliflora* (bumblebee orchid).

You reach **Paderne Castle** (Picnic 13) in **37min**. From one side of the castle there are open views towards Paderne, but the other side looks down on the fascinating arched bridge which was part of an old route. We go there next. As you face the front of the castle, leave by a small path which follows the left side of the castle; at first you are looking down over the old bridge. The path does not descend imme-diately, but contours up-river and away from the bridge. After three

Paderne Castle was conquered in 1249, during the reign of Don Afonso III, but history does not record whether the battle was fierce and bloody or whether the castle was damaged.

In 1305 it was given by Don Dinis to the Master of the Order of Aviz, Don Lorenço Annes, suggesting that the castle was still in use in that period. Today only the outer walls remain sufficiently intact to remind us of its past grandeur. Much of the interior has been destroyed, although there are still some remains of the chapel dedicated to Our Lady of the Ascension.

The nearby high-arched bridge spanning the river is believed to date from an earlier period, from Roman times, when the river was navigable. It was rebuilt sometime in the Middle Ages, probably by the Crusaders, and it has survived the ravages of time remarkably well.

minutes, the path goes left and descends to the river. You meet a strong crossing path by the riverside (**43min**). *(A right here returns to the 30min point.)* Follow the path downstream towards the bridge, with the river on the right. *Arundo donax*, the giant reed, grows tall by the river, while the dwarf fan palm, *Chamaerops humilis*, is at home in the arid ground on the other side of the path.

The BRIDGE is reached in **51min**. Cross it and turn left. *(The return route enters from the right here, and this is where Short walk 4 turns right.)* At first continue along the river but, in just over a minute, take the strong path uphill to the right — a steady climb. Near the top, the path veers right towards a ruin. Before reaching the ruin, turn left on a rising path which meets a faint field track coming from the ruin. Turn left on this track, back across the top of the valley you just climbed. The track becomes more distinct as it bends to the right. Much of the climbing is over in **1h06min** and, as you start to descend a little, there are wider views to enjoy through the almond groves.

Turn left when you reach a T-junction (**1h12min**; *the Alternative walk goes right here*). Two minutes later, turn right at a T of tracks. Head for the bridge over the motorway, keeping a corrugated iron building over to your right. Once over the MOTORWAY BRIDGE, continue ahead. When the track swings away to the right (**1h20min**), keep ahead on an earthen track, which soon becomes a walled-in trail. Ignore a path forking right (a short-cut, but it is overgrown), but, at a T-junction, follow the trail to the right. Then (**1h30min**) swing left between houses into a rough tarmac road. Reach a narrow road at a T-junction (**1h32min**) and turn right, to meet a wider road (**1h33min**). Keep ahead here. *(Short walk 2 goes left and meets the Albufeira/ Paderne road at Cerro do Ouro almost immediately.)*

Follow the road back under the motorway and towards the river. Turn right up a track, to an old WINDMILL (**1h45min**). The machinery is still in place, but take care if you venture inside — it looks in danger of collapsing. Fine views are on offer, with the hills to the north drawing the eye. Return to the road and turn right. The castle comes into view ahead (**1h52min**) as you reach a crossroads. Follow the road to the left here, skirting a white farmhouse on the right. Cross the MOTORWAY BRIDGE, and stay left (**1h56min**). As the castle comes into view again, you pass beneath a SIGN, 'AZENHA', and the road reverts to track. Very soon (**1h59min**), take a path down to the right; it cuts a bend off the track and descends to an OLD MILL (AZENHAL;

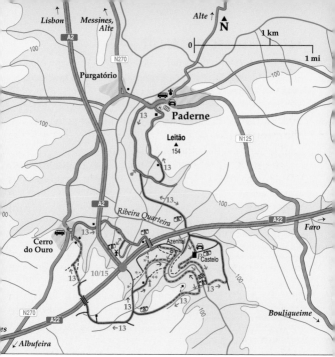

2h01min). (The track sweeps down to the river just *beyond* this mill, where *Short walk 4 and the Alternative walk both rejoin the main walk.*)

Turn right to continue past the mill* on a riverside path, beside paper-white *Narcissus papyraceus* (photograph page 121) and colonies of the Spanish bluebell, *Endymion hispanicus*. Cross the BRIDGE (**2h14min**) and turn right on a field track *(Short walk 3 rejoins here.)* Or turn left and follow the path by the river back to the 30min-point. The path soon becomes a badly-eroded track. Climb to a cross-track (**2h19min**) and turn left. Stay with the main track as you crest the small hill and start to descend. When you join the track to the castle (**2h24min**), keep right downhill. Ignore the track joining from the right four minutes later. On reaching your outward route (**2h29min**), turn right under the MOTORWAY. *(Short walk 1 rejoins here.)* Back at the T-junction near the *fonte* on the left (**2h44min**), turn right. In three minutes, take a rough track up left, which becomes surfaced on reaching a house on the left. When you come to some apartments (**3h**), keep around to the right. Pass a SCHOOL on the left, descend to the CEMETERY, and turn right to the STADIUM in **Paderne** (**3h05min**).

*If the river is low here, the walk can be shortened by crossing the WEIR and retracing the outward route from the 30min-point.

14 MONTE SECO CIRCUIT

Distance: 9.5km/6mi; 2h02min

Grade: Moderate. There are two short sections of steep uphill walking and a stony descent to the riverside. The diversion to the trig point adds 0.8km/0.5mi and 10min to the main walk total.

Equipment: See pages 44-45.

How to get there: 🚗 only accessible by car: Take the N270 Boliqueime to Loulé road. Soon after crossing over the A22 motorway at Junction 11 and passing a quarry on the left, turn left towards Parragil (shown as Gilvrazino on many maps). At the T-junction in Parragil turn left again. Then keep ahead at crossroads (still in Parragil): from here it is 3.5km/2.2mi to Ribeira de Algibre; park where the houses end.

Shorter walks

1 Ribeira de Algibre — Monte Seco hamlet — Ribeira de Algibre (7.5km/4.7mi; 1h38min). Moderate, with only one short section of uphill walking. Follow the main walk to the 27min-point. Keep ahead now to continue along the contour of the hill, passing a white house below on the right. Ignore tracks left and right. In 32min, there is a fine well on the left, as the track describes a U round the head of a gully. Keep ahead, ignoring tracks forking right (at 34min and 40min). When you reach a T-junction (48min), turn right downhill, picking up the main walk at the 1h12min-point.

2 Algibre Valley (8km/5mi; 1h40min). Easy, level track-walking. Start along the main walk and go right at the first junction, then fork right in 15min. Keep along this track, ignoring side-tracks, as it meanders along the Ribeira de Algibre, never far from the river over to the right. In 36min you pass the point where the main walk enters from the left (the

Poppy fields near the Ribeira de Algibre

1h26min-point in the main walk). Continue to where you can easily get down to the river (about 50min — beyond the cultivated fields, where the track forks right). The walk can be as long or short as you like; just return the same way.

3   Ribeira de Algibre — Monte Seco hamlet — Ribeira de Algibre (3.2km/2mi; 40min). Easy. Follow the main walk to the 19min-point, then return down the track on the right. Ignore a track up to the right, but turn right further on (28min). Ten minutes later, pass your outgoing field track up to the right and continue left, to cross the diagonal field track. Return to the walled-in track and follow it back to the start.

S et in the hills and valleys of the limestone Barrocal (see Walk 11), this is a scenic country circuit in any season, but especially interesting to wild flower lovers in spring. *Paeonia broteroi* (photograph page 121) and poppies are amongst the showy flowers on the lower sections, while the seemingly-dry hillsides abound with wild orchids.

Start the walk in the HAMLET of **Ribeira de Algibre**: turn left (west) along the track on the south (Parragil) side of the BRIDGE. At the crossing of tracks soon reached, go diagonally left. *(Or right for Shorter walk 2.)* Shortly, as the main track swings right, stay ahead up a field track. An old THRESHING FLOOR is just to the right; ignore a track forking right just beyond it. Now in a steady uphill climb, the track bends right to eventually pass a track joining from the left (**9min**). Stay ahead, uphill, to run into a concrete road five minutes later. Keep ahead into an open area, and descend to the centre of **Monte Seco** (**19min**), where a left turn meets the main road. *(The track to the right is the return route of Short walk 3.)* Opposite is the local, authentic café/bar/shop (to the left is another café/bar); aside from Ribeira de Algibre, these are the only places for refreshments on the walk. Turn right here and right again less than a minute later, on a narrow road. When this road soon reverts to track, keep ahead. There are extensive views over the Algibre Valley as this high-level track undulates round the hill. Just short of the top of a sharp rise, not far before a white house below on the right (**27min**), turn left uphill on a track. *(Shorter walk 1 continues ahead here.)*

Stay on this track in a steady ascent towards the summit of **Monte Seco**. Walled enclosures pattern the valley to the right. Monte Seco's trig point, over to the left, is marked by a mobile phone mast. The track soon swings away from the trig point and descends to a T-junction (**44min**), where the main walk turns right. From this position, the trig point is easily seen back to the left. (To reach the TRIG POINT on **Monte Seco** (296m/971ft), a

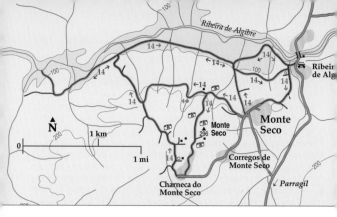

panoramic viewpoint, turn *left* here, towards a deserted farmhouse. In two minutes, turn left through a wide gap in a stone wall and head diagonally across to the trig point — this takes five minutes).

The track wends its way down between buildings, to meet a narrow surfaced road (**50min**). Turn right uphill; the road reverts to a high-level track in under four minutes. At a junction (**55min**), go right on a rising track, which leads to a house less than two minutes later. Stay ahead here up a walled-in trail, passing a circular THRESHING FLOOR on the right. Reach a staggered junction of tracks (**1h**) and turn left. Deserted hamlets, almond and olive groves feature in the landscape along this very pleasant route. Do not be tempted to stray down right when the trail becomes a field track for a short distance; it soon reverts back to a walled-in trail. When you reach a T-junction in **1h05min**, turn right (north).

As the track starts to descend, Monte Seco's trig point can be seen again, across the valley to the right. Where a track goes left (**1h09min**), keep straight downhill. Care is needed now, as the track becomes quite stony. Across the valley ahead lies Espargal, while a line of giant *Arundo donax* reeds in the valley floor marks the bed of the Algibre River. Pass a track on the right (**1h12min**). *(Shorter walk 1 rejoins here.)* Nine minutes later, ignore a minor track to the right; continue downhill. The track swings right, almost parallel with the river below to the left, before heading left to the valley floor and a T-junction of tracks (**1h26min**). Turn right here *(left is the outward route of Shorter walk 2)*.

There is chance to relax now as the track meanders through delightful countryside, following the line of the **Ribeira de Algibre** on the left. When you reach a junction (**1h50min**) go left, following the river over left, back to the HAMLET of **Ribeira de Algibre** (**2h02min**).

104

15 PENINA CIRCUIT

See map pages 108-109   **Distance:** 8km/5mi; 1h32min

Grade: moderate. Rocha da Pena peaks at 479m/1571ft and the starting point is 300m/984ft, so there is little climbing. Apart from a stretch of stony track on the descent to Penina, the paths and tracks are generally good. Jeep safaris, in high season, can make the track between Penina and the *fonte* very dusty.

How to get there and return: 🚗 only accessible by car. Travelling from Pena towards Salir on the N124, turn north at Taipa (1km short of Salir), following signs for Rocha da Pena and Alcaria. After passing through Alcaria, turn left towards Rocha da Pena. Keep ahead and park where the road ends at the Fonte dos Amoados in Rocha, or alongside the wide track just beyond it. (*Note:* An environmental centre in Pena village is worth a stop. It is located on the N124 in the old school at the west end of the village. This walk can be easily started from Penina as well.)

Longer walk: Windmill circuit and trig point (8.6km/5.3mi; 2h12min). Moderate. Park as for the main walk. Follow the main walk as far as the trig point (50min). Then return to the circular clearing and pick up the notes for the *Alternative walk* from the 19min-point.

Alternative ascent via the windmills (8km/5mi; 1h44min). Moderate-difficult; a more challenging route for fit and agile walkers from the 36min-point, but a pleasant short easy return walk from the *fonte* to the windmills. Start from the *fonte:* walk along the road towards Pena, but fork left immediately onto the diagonal rising track. In 14min cross a minor track, to reach the windmills (16min). Return to the track crossing and turn right uphill. As the track levels out (19min), turn back sharp left uphill. In under a minute, just as the rough field track starts to descend, turn right uphill on a path. After a few minutes the main path, which rises ahead gradually, becomes faint and is easily missed. (Be aware of an unseen quarry downhill to the left.) You may find yourself on a more obvious route not far to the right of it: this becomes a scramble, at first rising gently, but then more steeply as you approach the top. Once on top, head left to reach a circular clearing (35min), and pick up the notes from the 19min-point in the main walk to continue.

Alternative walk: Windmill circuit (3.6km/2.3mi; 55min). Moderate, but a tricky section down the hillside to the windmills requires careful footwork. Park as for the main walk. Follow the main walk to the 19min-point (the circular clearing). Continue ahead on the track beyond the clearing, and take the path forking right (23min). (The strong onward path leads to the end of the ridge and a very steep and

Picnic 15 is set close to the weathered limestone face of Rocha da Pena, seven minutes from the start of the walk. Nearby the wild peony, Paeonia broterei, is profuse, and its red blooms (photograph page 121) can be seen from February through to May.

tricky descent.) This route traverses the hillside more gradually after an initial steep section. *Take care* not to stray off the route to the right, as there is an unseen steep drop into a quarry. Continue ahead as a strong path joins from the left, and keep on downhill, to emerge on a field track. Go left here, meet another track (35min) and turn right. You reach a stabilised track two minutes later, where you turn left to the windmills (40min). Enjoy the fine views, then return along the track which gradually descends the hillside back to the *fonte*.

This is another walk through the Barrocal limestones of Algarve (see Walk 11 for more details), but only on the diversion to the summit of Rocha da Pena do you encounter the scrub-type vegetation, or *matos*, typical of this region. Outside the Barrocal, the *matos* is very different, and some of the characteristic plants are mentioned in Walk 18 (see second paragraph on page 118).

Although it ranges over the same botanically-rich limestone ridge (now a conservation area) described in earlier editions of the book, we have since changed the original walk, to take into account a newly-waymarked route. This crosses the ridge in a westerly direction and circles back through the village of Penina. Our original route — up to the ridge, eastwards to the ruined windmills and down to the track — was a favourite of many walkers. It is still viable and described above as the Alternative walk. The really energetic can do *both* walks, making a figure of eight!

Start the walk from the **Fonte dos Amoados** in **Rocha**, where you park the car. The route to Rocha da Pena is SIGNPOSTED AND WAYMARKED up to the right, on the far side of the café. The ascent is steep for the first few minutes, then the incline lessens, as you enter an area of light woodland. An area shaded by carob trees (Picnic 15; **7min**) enjoys fine views over the farmed countryside. Stay on the track as it swings right, to continue under the cliffs of Rocha da Pena, and slip into a gentler pace to counter the steady ascent. Level stretches give some respite, but the open views to the right are distraction enough to make this section pass quickly. At the top of the hill (**19min**) you reach a circular clearing.

The onward route up to the trig point on the summit starts here. Look for the waymarked path leaving the clearing, immediately to the left of where you entered it, and follow it westwards. (*But for the Alternative walk go straight ahead.*) The well-defined path keeps more or less to the left-hand edge of the ridge top.

In **29min** the path descends the extreme left-hand edge of a NEOLITHIC STONE BANK which extends across the ridge.

SCRUBLAND

Looking ahead, pick out the cleared area below the final rise to the summit. This is reached in **40min**. Cross the clearing and walk up a track. The trig point is now over to the left. As the track starts to descend slightly, take the WAYMARKED PATH off left up to the TRIG POINT on **Rocha da Pena** (**50min**), from where you will have commanding views.

Return from the trig point to the track and turn left to continue. The track now heads down the end of the ridge before curling left towards Penina. As the track descends, *take care;* a section of loose stones underfoot makes walking tricky for a short distance. Once past a minor track running in from the left (**1h 02min**), the track surface improves on the final descent into Penina.

Enter **Penina** (**1h09min**) and head downhill into the centre of this typical rural village. In just over a minute, turn left (waymarked) where there is a FOUNTAIN on the upper corner to the right. Take the third village street on the right, to pass a café on the left, then turn left at the T-junction soon reached. Immediately on leaving Penina (**1h 12min**), turn left on a track and, half a minute later, at a three-way junction, turn right on a trail. The trail runs besides a long building on the right, then reverts to path as it skirts a field. In **1h17min** the path emerges on a track, at a bend. (Down to the right is the Penina to Pena road.) Keep ahead on the wide stabilised track now, parallel with Rocha da Pena ridge over to the left. The way undulates through pleasant and tranquil countryside back to the **Fonte dos Amoados** (**1h32min**).

SCRUBLAND is an important type of vegetation in the Mediterranean. But despite many common elements, the scrub is named differently throughout the region. To the east of the Iberian Peninsula, the term *macchie* or *maquis* refers to the tall scrubland, where the shrubs stand about the height of man or more, and *phrygana* or *garrigue* is used for the knee-high, more open scrubland. The Portuguese use one term for both: *matos*; similarly, the Spanish use *mattoral*. The plant communities which make up the *matos* are a good indication of the underlying geology and are especially easy to 'read' in Algarve, to determine whether you are in the Barrocal region or not. The holly oak, *Quercus coccifera* (photograph above), the shrubby wild olive, *Olea europaea*, the wild jasmine, *Jasminium fruticans*, the white small-flowered cistus, *Cistus monspeliensis*, and the dwarf fan palm, *Chamaerops humilis*, are a few of the many plants which reliably indicate the presence of limestone.

16 SALIR CIRCUIT

Distance: 11.0km/6.8mi; 2h15min

Grade: easy-moderate. The walk uses mainly good (although occasion-ally stony) tracks and paths; there is very little climbing involved.

Note: At some times of year, it may be difficult to cross the Rio Seco (52min-point in the main walk). If so, return to the 49min-point and go right along the track. In three minutes, cross a stream on stepping stones and in a further four minutes cross the Rio Seco on stepping stones. The white house at the 1h15min-point in the walk is ahead to the left; the track passes behind it, then swings left to the road. (If the Seco here is too deep, go along the grassy track left (north) before reaching the river. Follow this to a field which you skirt to the right. Descend a steep path back to the river and walk alongside it, to rejoin the main walk along the road. A left turn soon leads to the 1h21min-point.)

Equipment: See pages 44-45.

How to get there and return: 🚗 only accessible by car. See details in Car tour 3, page 29. Leave the car on the south side of Salir, near where the main road bends right to descend towards Loulé.

Shorter circuit: Salir — Arneiro — Salir (9.2km/5.7mi; 1h50min). Grade as main walk. Follow the main walk to the 47min-point. Do not turn right, but stay ahead on the stabilised track. When you meet the main road 12 minutes later, cross straight over onto a track signposted 'Pedras Ruivas'. Pick up the main walk again at the 1h21min-point.

Even within the confines of the large valley around Salir, there is an unexpected variety in the landscape that can only be appreciated if you are on foot. This walk follows some narrow footpaths, bounded by groves, and broad tracks through wilder regions; it crosses rivers on stepping stones and visits intimate farming communities. We return to the church in the centre of Salir; this is a spectacular viewpoint with an adjacent café/bar and picnic area. We also visit the old castle area shown overleaf, before heading back to the car.

Start the walk at the PARKING PLACE in **Salir**: continue to the right and head down the LOULÉ ROAD towards the river and the bridge (PONTE DE SALIR). In **8min**, just before the

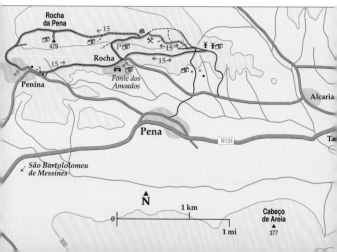

bridge, turn left on a track. As you approach a farm four minutes later, head first for the entrance to the farmyard, then swing left to take a path through olive and carob groves. The path follows a LINE OF POSTS carrying a cable. Ignore paths right and left. For a moment it looks as though the path finishes at a house (**16min**), but stay ahead past the house. Head left uphill and cross a field track. The path then leads around to the left and meets a field track/path (**19min**); go right here. When you meet another track, go left to a narrow road, where you turn right. As you ascend gently, keep an eye on the roadside vegetation: you might spot the peony, *Paeonia broteroi*, which graces the early months with its elegant red flowers (photograph page 121).

As you reach the top of the rise (**25min**), turn left towards 'FUJANCA'. (Note the stone cross on the wall of the house here.) Then turn right just past the house, on a track. This track runs through the orange and almond groves shown overleaf. Pass a track off left, then meet a track on a bend (**30min**); keep straight on here. Stay with this slightly elevated track, enjoying the views across the valley to the left. Ignore all side tracks until the main track bends left and starts into a deeper descent (**47min**). Just past this point, two tracks join from the right. *(Keep straight ahead here on the main stabilised track, if you are doing the Shorter circuit).* Take the second of these, a rough track. Descend gradually through farmed land; keep ahead as the main track goes left (**49min**).

The first of TWO RIVERS is met in **52min**, and there are just enough stones for you to step across to continue along the track opposite. This leads to a much stonier river, reached four minutes later. Cross this one by heading diagonally right, and join a walled-in track which climbs

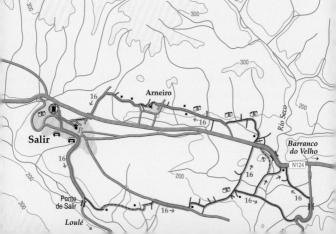

up and around to the left, affording views back down over the river before the SURFACED ROAD is reached in **1h**.

Turn left down the road, cross the bridge five minutes later, and take a track off left almost immediately. The track leads at first through once-cultivated land, now reverting to *matos*. After crossing a small stream bed (**1h11min**), the track leads diagonally left; then it swings to the right, towards the road and a white house. (The alternative track, used when the Rio Seco is high, enters from the left here; see 'Note' at the top of page 108.) Pass in front of the house to reach the SALIR ROAD (**1h15min**). Turn left downhill along the road and cross the bridge over the **Rio Seco**. (The second 'high water' option, a grassy track, come in here from the left.) Ignore the first track off right just past the bridge; take the *second* sharp right (**1h21min**), signposted 'PEDRAS RUIVAS', just before a house and farm. *(The Shorter circuit rejoins here.)* After only a minute along this track, fork left, then fork left again (**1h23min**), before rising uphill through the cork oaks. The track swings left below a square white house and shortly gives you the first views of the white tower by the church in Salir. Descend to meet a narrow road and turn right.

There is a different character to the walk now, as you weave your way back to Salir through a succession of hamlets, taking a course roughly parallel with the main road below left. Stay ahead to enjoy views over the picturesque valley on your left — and Rocha da Pena (Walk 15) slightly to the right. Eventually you reach the hamlet of **Arneiro** (**1h43min**). At the junction, go ahead up a steep concrete trail between houses. When you meet a road on a bend, follow it straight ahead and into a field track (**1h44min**). This track swings down left; keep ahead here, on a path (alongside a building on the left). When the path joins another field track (**1h46min**), keep ahead. Stay right at the fork and soon meet a concrete road. Turn right to continue through a farmyard. Continue along the concrete road as it dips and rises, to pass through another farmyard. At a T-junction (**1h 55min**), turn left towards Salir and soon bend right to another T-junction Then turn left again to head directly towards Salir.

As you join the MAIN ROAD (**1h58min**), turn right and then immediately left, up the road signposted to 'SALIR' and 'CASTELO'. Turn right just a minute later, to follow a surfaced track up towards a higher road (**2h01min**), where you turn right and then left shortly afterwards. You come to the CHURCH and SQUARE on the pinnacle of the

Narrow lane leading to the castle ramparts in Salir. Note the typical Algarvian chimney. Below: almond groves near Salir

hill (**2h05min**). There is a superb panorama from this excellent viewpoint, which you can enjoy from a seat in the shade — perhaps with a drink from the café. Nearby is a small PARK area with seating (Picnic 16). Our advice is not to picnic here before midday since, while the chimes of the church clock are pleasing from a distance, it's more like a sonic boom close by!

Leave the square the way you entered it* and continue ahead (passing the road by which you arrived) through old Salir, to find the remains of the CASTLE. The second cobbled street on the right (**2h09min**; see photograph above), leads you up to the old ramparts. You can walk along them by swinging right and continuing around to the left, to complete a circle taking just four minutes, bringing you back to the 2h09min-point, but this time facing the church. Turn right downhill to head back to the car, taking a left turn and then a second left, to get onto the road and back to the PARKING PLACE (**2h15min**).

*Or, for a speedy return to your car, leave the square down the steps at the side of the park. Turn left along the village street, then follow it as it bends right to the Loulé road and the start of the walk.

17 ESTÓI • GUILHIM • FIALHO • ESTÓI

See also photograph page 27

Distance: 15.0km/9.4mi; 3h20min

Grade: moderate — mainly on good tracks and paths, with occasional stony and difficult sections. The longest climb is to the top of Guilhim at 313m/1026ft.

Equipment: See pages 44-45.

How to get there: 🚌 by bus from Faro to Estói (*warning:* not all buses enter Estói; be sure to refer to Timetable 6). Journey time 20min. 🚗 by car: see Car tour 3, pages 26-27. Park in Estói or at Milreu.

To return: 🚌 bus from Estói to Faro (Timetable 6), or 🚗 by car

Short walks: All are moderate.

1 Milreu — Guilhim — Milreu (6.9m/4.3mi; 1h52min). 🚌 or 🚗 to Milreu. Follow the main walk from the 14min-point to the obelisk on the top of Guilhim and the road below (the 1h18min-point in the main walk). Go right here and stay on this road, passing an old windmill in 10 minutes (the diversion to inspect it adds 0.8km/0.5mi). Ignore the track joining from the right two minutes later (where Short walk 2 joins). You meet the intersection with your outward route six minutes later (the 34min-point in the main walk). Turn left into the trail, to continue back to Milreu.

2 Milreu — Guilhim — Milreu (7.2km/4.5mi; 1h40min). 🚌 or 🚗 to Milreu. Follow the main walk from the 14min-point to the obelisk on the top of Guilhim and return the same way, until you reach the end of the track which was first encountered at the 1h-point in the main walk. Turn left downhill here, then turn sharp right on meeting a road seven minutes later. Stay ahead and come back to the intersection with your outward route six minutes later (the 34min-point in the main walk). Turn left to continue back to Milreu.

3 Milreu — Guilhim — Milreu (9.3mi/6.1mi; 2h08min). 🚌 or 🚗 to Milreu. Follow the main walk from the 14min-point to the Bordeira road (the 1h55min-point in the main walk). Then, instead of crossing the bridge, follow the track straight ahead. This leads (in 20 minutes) back to the 26min-point in the main walk. Turn left here, to continue back to Milreu. (This short-cut passes a quarry, where it can be very dusty for about five minutes, if a lorry passes.)

4 Estói — Guilhim — Fialho (10.9km/6.9mi; 2h31min). Follow the main walk to the Faro road at Fialho (2h36min), where you can catch a bus.

5 Estói — Fialho — Estói (11.8km/7.3mi; 2h16min). Follow the main walk to the 26min-point. Turn right at this junction and follow the track past a quarry (see 3 above). You join a narrow surfaced road 19 minutes later, where you turn right to cross a bridge and meet the Bordeira road in a minute. From here pick up the main walk (at the 1h50min-point).

Estói has two special points of interest, the ruins of a Roman villa (Milreu) near the start of the walk, and the Palacio do Visconde de Estói at the end. The villa dates back to about the first or second century BC and is thought to have survived until the eighth century AD. The excavations show a bathing complex still with some mosaic work, as well as foundations of houses and the apse of a Roman temple. The 18th-century palace is private prop-

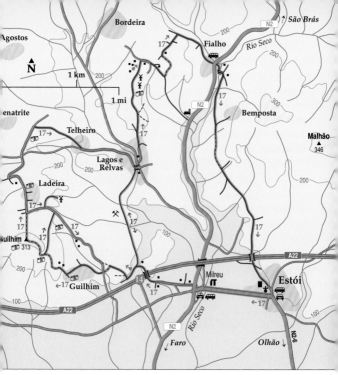

erty, but the gardens (photograph page 27) are open to the public and are curious enough to be interesting. This walk leaves Estói by the bridge over Rio Seco, to head first for the viewpoint on the summit of Guilhim. Taking a northerly route, a broad ridge is followed for a time. This leads you through areas of cultivation, before you eventually curve around to Fialho and cross the Rio Seco again.

Leave the bus, or park, in **Estói**. **Start the walk** by heading away from Estói, back towards the main FARO/SÃO BRÁS ROAD. Visit **Milreu** en route (closed Mondays). Cross the main road diagonally (**14min**), into the minor road to the right of the surfaced road opposite, and walk straight into rural surroundings where the ubiquitous yellow Bermuda buttercup brightens the way, and where scattered farm houses add interest to this area of cultivation. Keep ahead as far as the junction reached in **22min**; here turn right and cross the BRIDGE OVER THE MOTORWAY. Once over, descend to a T-junction (**26min**) and turn left. *(Short walks 1, 2 and 3 return to this point, and you turn right here for Short walk 5.)* You reach a WELL in about **27min**.

Continue along the surfaced track, which rises above the motorway slip-road down left. About two minutes later, at the top of the rise, turn right to continue on a rough track, heading in the direction of Guilhim. Keep right towards the hill at the fork. The track reverts to path; stay left at a fork, to meet a narrow surfaced road (**34min**; *Short walks 1 and 2 come in from the right here*). Continue ahead along a track; it soon leads through the HAMLET of **Guilhim**.

The views open up to the east — towards Olhão and the mound of São Miguel, easily distinguished by the mast on the top. Reach a cross track (**42min**) and turn right up the rough concrete. In a few minutes, when the concrete ends at a couple of houses, stay ahead on a field track. The track swings left uphill and continues along the contours, becoming more a trail, then a path. It rises into old olive grove terraces. There are sweeping views left towards the coast before the path heads up to the right (**50min**) and leaves the terraces behind.

You rise onto the end of a track. *(Short walk 2 returns from the obelisk on Guilhim to this point before heading down the track.)* As you catch a breath here, you can enjoy extensive views — from São Miguel in the east to Faro in the south. Continue by crossing the track and walking uphill on a path which soon leads left along the ridge towards the obelisk. Much of the climbing is over now, and all that remains is to follow the path through the *matos,* to reach the OBELISK on **Guilhim** (**1h05min**). It

is a fantastic look-out point, with views stretching from the coast in the south to the ring of hills in the north.

With your back to the sea, follow the wide path which heads into a very steep descent. Keep ahead when the path runs into a road at a bend (**1h13min**; *but turn right here for Short walk 1*), and ignore tracks off left and right as you continue along the ridge through the cultivated farmlands shown below. At a crossing of roads/tracks (**1h20min**) swing right, still following the road — which now leaves cultivation to head down into the *matos*. Cross a surfaced road five minutes later, and join a wider surfaced road ahead. You catch distant views of Estói as you walk this section. Take the track off right, just as you start to descend (**1h31min**), and follow this rough track, to meet the road again some eight minutes later. Here turn left. Olive and carob trees provide shade from time to time as you wander down this pleasant country lane to a BRIDGE and the BORDEIRA ROAD (**1h50min**). *(The track off right here is used for Short walks 3 and 5.)*

Turn left here, in the direction of Bordeira (but note that there is a good café /restaurant to the right). Then take the narrow surfaced road on the right, only three minutes later. (Or first contine on the main road for another minute, to a café/bakery on the left, from where a path leads up the bank to this narrow road.) Continue as the road rises steeply, giving views of Estói to the right. In **2h**,

This walk passes through a region dotted with picturesque farms, like the one shown here (about 1h20min into the walk). Citrus fruits, olives, almonds, and carobs are commonly grown. The carob is no longer valued for its crop of beans, which was once used to feed the animals. However, these trees are still abundant throughout the area.

as the tar runs out, the main track swings round and down to the right. Keep straight on along a rough track here, heading towards a villa and a ruined windmill. At a junction of tracks/trails, follow the main track to the left, to cross over to the far side of the ridge. The track then swings right along the left-hand side of the ridge; you pass two ruined windmills and a villa on your right. The track then passes some buildings on the left. You emerge on a road (**2h14min**), where you turn right. Guilhim is now over to the right. Keep ahead on a track, as the road swings down to the right.

On reaching a fork that leads either side of a house (**2h17min**), go downhill to the right on an old track. Take care at the junction reached four minutes later, where the main track swings right, down towards a FACTORY on the main road, and a lesser track joins from the left. Turn left and, half a minute later, take the narrow walled-in trail ahead. Come to a house (**2h24min**) and skirt it to the left, keeping it to your right. Descend a rough track with two-wheel concrete strips. Ignore tracks off left and right; go right at the T-junction (**2h29min**). With a stream bed to your left, continue down to the main FARO/SÃO BRÁS ROAD at **Fialho** (**2h31min**). *(Those doing Short walk 4 can catch a bus back to Faro from here.)*

Cross the road to join a track on the far side which leads to a BRIDGE over the **Rio Seco** (**2h34min**). Cross the bridge; ignore the track off to the left, but fork down right (**2h36min**). The track roughly parallels the river, but rises steadily above it. Keep straight ahead when you rise to meet a track on a bend (**2h47min**).

Ignore the track joining from the left (**2h53min**), but take the left fork just over two minutes later. Estói comes into view, and soon the way is all descent. The track widens and passes a RETIREMENT HOME (**3h02min**). Walking through the intensely-cultivated environs of Estói, you catch glimpses of the old palace. After crossing a BRIDGE OVER THE MOTORWAY, keep ahead at a diagonal cross-tracks (**3h13min**), with the PALACE GROUNDS to the left. You walk beneath the bridge joining the palace to the formal gardens two minutes later, then pass the village WASH-HOUSE and FOUNTAIN (both on the left; **3h16min**). Take the first narrow street to the right, just before reaching the small square, and the stepped street to the right almost immediately. This leads to the PALACE GATES and MAIN SQUARE in **Estói** (**3h20min**), where the BUS stops.

18 SÃO BRÁS • TAREJA • VALE DE ESTACAS • SÃO BRÁS

Distance: 10.8km/6.7mi; 2h16min

Grade: easy-moderate. There is some climbing involved, through undulating countryside — but nothing excessive. The paths and tracks used are stony and difficult in some places.

Equipment: See pages 44-45.

How to get there: 🚌 by bus from Faro to São Brás (Timetable 6). Journey time 35min. 🚗 by car: park in the centre *(centro),* on the wide dual carriageway road (on the route of the walk), leading north from the main square and signposted 'Almargens'. It is easier to park near the 9min-point in the walk. On Saturdays (market day), one carriageway is closed, and the other temporarily reverts to two-way traffic.

To return: 🚌 bus from São Brás to Faro (Timetable 6), or 🚗 by car

Short walks: All three are easy-moderate.

1 São Brás — Tareja — São Brás (6.6km/4.1mi; 1h20min). Follow the main walk to the road just below the centre of Tareja (36min). Instead of turning left to the centre, keep ahead along the road, to reach a walled-in track on the right (39min; before the bridge and fountain). Follow the walled-in track and, at the end of the wall on the right (less than two minutes later), take the faint path off to the right (41min). Stay right, parallel with the wall on the right. The path leads left near the top of the field, then heads up right to a crossing track (45min). Turn right now, to link up with the outward route three minutes later (the 32min-point in the main walk). Now retrace your steps to São Brás.

2 São Brás — Tareja — São Brás (8.6km/5.3mi; 1h45min). Follow the main walk beyond Tareja, to the track met at the 54min-point. Turn right here (instead of left), and follow the track to a surfaced road near a bridge and a fountain down on the left (1h03min). Turn right here and, in just over a minute, turn left into a walled-in track. From here the route is the same as described in Short walk 1 above, so follow those notes from the 39min-point to return to São Brás.

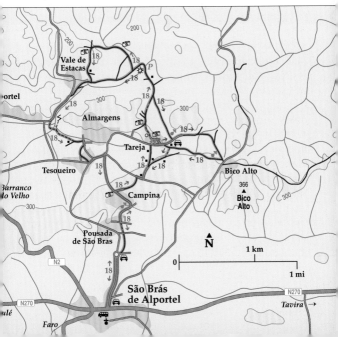

3   São Brás — Tareja — São Brás (8km/5mi; 1h38min). Follow the main walk to the road just below the centre of Tareja (36min). Instead of turning left to the centre a minute later, keep ahead along the road. The road reverts to track. When this main track swings up left (44min), stay ahead on a minor track. At the T of tracks (47min), turn right; three minutes later, turn right again, passing to the left of the well shown opposite. Ahead is Tareja. When you meet a wall on the left incorporating red ventilation bricks (1h), turn left on a faint path, with the wall on the right. Now pick up the notes for Short walk 1, at the 41min-point.

São Brás lies on the edge of the Barrocal, the limestone region. This walk leads through interesting pastoral landscapes to the village of Tareja and continues into a very different region — the schists of the northern *serras*.

Here the acidic soils support a *matos* which is very different from that in the limestone regions. Cistus dominates, particularly the large sticky-leaved *Cistus ladanifer*, which often covers the rolling hills. The large white flowers, sometimes blotched with dark red at the base of the petals, are short-lasting like all cistus and are never produced in sufficient numbers to smother the hillsides in blossom. Cork oaks too are present, as a reminder of an earlier time, when the vegetation consisted largely of oak forest with an undergrowth of cistus. Colour is added by the heaths — the white-flowered tree heather, *Erica lusitanica,* and the pink *Erica australis,* both of which have a prolonged flowering period, and by the dark blue lavender, *Lavandula stoechas.*

Start the walk from where you leave the bus in the main SQUARE in **São Brás**. Head up the wide DUAL CARRIAGEWAY road (also the location of the Saturday market) towards Almargens. In **9min**, at the small ROUND-ABOUT in the central reservation just before the end of the dual carriageway, turn right into a road and, almost immediately, go left up a track. A steady ascent begins, and the track rises to meet a narrow surfaced road. Cross the road to enter a walled-in track/path which rises to cross another surfaced road (**15min**). Still in steady ascent, take the narrow road opposite. The walled-in road continues round to the right into more open countryside. Views to the east here include the mound of São Miguel, with its tall mast.

Keep ahead as the road descends to a junction, by a WELL (**21min**), and turn left up the road, heading towards the brow of a hill. At the brow of the hill (**25min**), turn right on a road which becomes a walled-in track. You meet a surfaced road four minutes later, where you turn right. Enter a walled road on the left just a minute later, immediately past a building on the left-hand corner. At a fork (**32min**; *the return route for the Short walks joins from the right here*) take the downhill track to the left, between new houses. This soon leads behind a restaurant on the left. Come to a surfaced road (**36min**) and turn right. Turn sharp left a minute later into **Tareja**, passing the WASH-HOUSE on the left. *(But keep straight along the road for Short walk 1.)* The road leads to a T-junction (**38min**), where you turn left. From here there is a fine view to the

Short walk 3 passes this Moorish-style well with a wheel.

north over rolling hills and valleys; it is easy to see the strategic position of the village. Follow the road between the houses, until it swings right and ends a minute later. Continue on a footpath, climbing towards the ridge ahead, with views of *matos*-covered hillsides on the right and the valley already traversed on the left.

In **40min**, stay ahead on the path, past a THRESHING FLOOR on the left. The path leads towards a small plateau, once another threshing floor, on top of the ridge (**41min**). Carpets of *Romulea bulbocodium* display a variety of shades in their small lilac flowers here. Continue over the hill, to meet the bend of a narrow track which can be seen ahead (**42min**). Keep straight along this track, to head into the *matos*. Ignore two tracks coming in from the left, and stay ahead as the lesser track narrows to a path (often ploughed over). Descend to the main track — either by going straight ahead or by going downhill to the right at the left of a gully. Quickly meeting the main track, go left (**54min**). *(But turn right here for Short walk 2.)* Ignore the track that soon comes up on the right. Passing an OLD RUIN on the right, keep right at a track junction, to the RIVER (Picnic 18; **57min**). The river area is a fine picnic spot, brightened by paper-white narcissi and pink oleander.

Cross the river on stepping stones and follow the track round to the far side of the ruined WATERMILL. Rise away from the confluence of rivers, keeping the mill on your left. Continue ahead along the track for two minutes*, then go right on a rising track, towards a high FENCE. You pass a WATER HOLE in the compound on the right. When you reach the top, join a track coming in from the left and continue in the same direction. Follow the spine of a ridge through scattered cork oak plantations, ignoring all turn-offs.

Soon after the high point (**1h10min**), the track dips down into a hollow, where a track crosses. Turn left on this track, heading for a cluster of buildings (Vale de Estacas) which can be seen on the road below. You follow a small ridge and then descend its left flank towards a meadow. Keep on the track past a house on the left, and go right downhill at the junction immediately afterwards. (The track from the mill, mentioned in the footnote below, joins here.) Cross the river diagonally to the right on stepping stones and continue on a field track back to the

*An alternative is to continue along the track past the mill for 12 minutes, keeping the river over to your left; this leads to the 1h20min-point in the main walk.

riverbank, then go left alongside the river on a path. The path widens to a track as it leaves the riverbank. Keep ahead, as a track joins from the left, and meet the surfaced road at **Vale de Estacas** (**1h24min**).

Turn left, but then leave the road four minutes later (after passing an ELECTRICITY SUBSTATION on the left), to take a stony path on the left (by a crash barrier). This path slopes down to a stream and more paper-white narcissi. Cross the stream ahead and continue to the right in a gradual ascent. Keep ahead and pass to the left of a white house, from where you stay ahead on the walled-in trail.

Keep left at the point where a track joins from the right (**1h 35min**) and continue along this track. When you meet a surfaced road a minute later, turn right, and turn right again almost immediately, into a track. As you rise to a cluster of houses (**Tesoueiro**), where the road is surfaced (**1h 40min**), turn left and left again to continue. Ignore the road immediately on the left; keep ahead to a crossroads (**1h47min**), where you turn right uphill. The track on the left at the top of the rise (**1h51min**) was the 25min-point in your outward route; keep straight on here to retrace your steps to **São Brás** (**2h16min**).

Top to bottom: Narcissus papyraceus *(paper-white narcissus)*, Paeonia broteroi, Convolvulus tricolor

19 TAVIRA NATIONAL FOREST

Distance: 8.0km/5mi; 1h48min

Grade: easy-moderate. The walk, mainly on tracks, is fairly easy going, apart from a tricky descent to cross the river towards the end. The only significant climbing is up to the trig point.

Equipment: See pages 44-45.

How to get there and return: 🚗 only accessible by car. Travelling eastwards on the N125 from the Faro direction, look for the large 'Euro-tel', some 3km beyond the bridge at Tavira. Turn left 400m beyond the hotel, on a road signposted 'Mata de Conceição'. Swing right in 600m, to cross the bridge over the stream, and continue ahead. Keep left at a junction (2.9km from the main road). Go under the motorway; then park in the open area (4.7km from the main road); a house is up to the left and there is a forest map board.

Shorter walks

1 Car parking area — ruins — car parking area (5km/3.1mi; 1h05min). Easy. Follow the main walk through the cutting (28min). Two minutes later, just before some ruins on the left, turn right on a crossing path. Follow this path along a winding valley. At a faint fork, go left to cross the stream, to continue with it on your right. Head up the valley, keeping to the right of the woodland. In seven minutes you rise up to a track; cross it and join a track directly opposite. Go down this grassy track. In 17 minutes you reach the outward route at the ford, from where you return to your car.

2 Car parking area — trig point diversion — car parking area (5.7km/3.5mi; 1h30min). Easy-moderate. Follow the main walk to the cutting (28min), then take the track off right immediately beyond it. Continue up this track for six minutes, until you reach another track entering from the left. Keep ahead here. You have rejoined the main walk at the 53min-point: follow it to the end, omitting the ascent to the trig point (Asseiceira). If you climb to the trig point, add 1km/0.6mi; 20min.

3 Car parking area — Malhada — Daroeira — car parking area (6.5km/4.0mi; 1h21min). Easy. Follow the main walk to the track junction at the 53min-point. Then turn right instead of left and, a minute later, take the grassy track on the left. Within ten minutes this takes you down to the river ford first reached at the 17min-point in the main walk. From here retrace your steps back to the car.

The Mata de Conceição is not the grand forest region that its name suggests, but merely a fairly large plantation of eucalyptus trees. Our walk quickly takes you through the forest and into the pleasing countryside beyond it. The *matos*-covered hills hiding small villages seem to roll timelessly away, creating an extremely photogenic landscape, given a clear day and a touch of colour in the countryside.

Start out from the CAR PARKING AREA at the **Mata de Conceição**: continue northeast along the surfaced road. After **3min** turn left on a surfaced road towards MALHADA DO PERES. Stay ahead on a track as the road swings off right (**4min**). Keep ahead at the junction of tracks reached in **7min**. Now in gentle descent, the track soon winds down

Crossing the river on stepping stones near Malhada do Peres

to a T-junction (a left turn here leads to a pleasant river-side picnic spot in two minutes). Turn *right* here, to a ford over the **Ribeira da Gafa** (**17min**). Cross on stones and continue on the track beyond *(the return route for Short walks 1 and 3 is the field track on the right here)*. Follow the main track up from the river, leaving the forest behind, to enjoy more open views. Look up to the right now, to see the trig point on top of Asseiceira; it is almost hidden by a pink villa. *Take note of this now,* because the villa obscures it completely later in the walk.

There is some climbing involved now, until you reach a CUTTING (**28min**). Beyond here you get your first real taste of the panoramic views which can be enjoyed throughout much of the rest of the walk. Ignore the track off right just beyond the cutting *(but turn right here for*

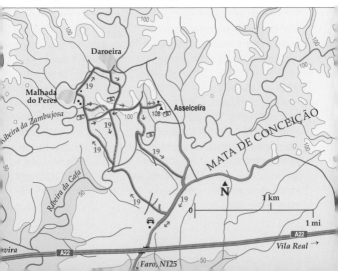

Short walk 2). The village of Malhada can be seen below to the left. The track leads past some RUINS on the left two minutes later. *(Short walk 1 leaves the main walk just before these ruins, along the path to the right.)* A junction of tracks is reached in **35min**. Turn right here, passing the remains of a round hut *(palheiro)* on the right, and heading towards the village of Daroeira, which soon comes into view. Continue ahead where a small river, the **Ribeira da Zambujosa**, crosses the track (use the stepping stones; **40min**). Then turn right at the track junction reached a minute later. **Daroeira** is close by on the left now, but it is soon left behind, when you bear right at the next track junction (**44min**). A brief ascent here sees you climbing above the Zambujosa, which is now on the right, only to descend to re-cross it in **47min**.

The walk takes on a different pastoral ambience for a time, as you climb steeply away from the river. Looking back as you ascend, there are some fine views over the village of Daroeira. Turn left when you meet another track at the top of the hill (**53min**. *(But go right for Short walk 3.)* You enjoy more good views from this high level track. As you near the trig point (obscured by the villa), turn right (**59min**) onto a rough track, heading down between two CAROB TREES. The diversion to the trig point starts as you reach these carobs. From here descend the narrow gully to the left, in the direction of the trig point, taking great care over the stony ground. From the bottom of the gully, head up to the trig point, taking the line between the *matos* on the right and the almond grove on the left, keeping to the left of the villa. From the TRIG POINT on **Asseiceira** (108m/355ft; **1h09min**) there is a fine panorama.

Return to the two carob trees by the side of the track, then bear left down the stony track towards the valley. The track leads along a saddle (**1h23min**) and bends left; your onward track can be seen to the right, on the far side of the river. Leave the saddle in the dip, by taking a strong path down to the right, towards a field below. Walk across the field to the right, heading towards the river, reached four minutes later. Go left along the riverbank, to descend to water level. You can cross the river on stepping stones at the point where it makes a loop. Then walk back along the riverbank and rise up right to a track. Follow this back up into the forest, keeping left at a fork. When you join the surfaced road (**1h40min**), turn right. Then turn right again at a junction. This road leads back to the CAR PARKING AREA (**1h48min**).

20 CASTRO MARIM NATURE RESERVE

Distance: 11.6km/7.2mi; 2h15min

Grade: moderate. This walk is virtually flat, which can be very tiring over a long distance. A section of footpath near the end of the walk can be slippery and demands some agility. A walk for bird-watchers. *NB:* Between the 1h32min- and 1h57min-points the walk can be slippery and treacherous after heavy rain, and is best not attempted in such conditions.

Equipment: See pages 44-45.

How to get there: 🚌 by bus from Faro to Vila Real de Santo António (Timetable 8). Journey time 1h40min. Or 🚆 by train from Faro to Vila Real (Timetable 9). Journey time, depending on the number of stops, from 1h18min to 1h44min. Then take a taxi to the start of the walk (3km; see parking notes for motorists). 🚗 by car: Castro Marim lies just to the northwest of Vila Real; see Car tour 4 (page 34) for details of how to get there. Park by a ruined building down the track to the left, some 1.6km/1mi after turning north onto the N122 from the main N125 immediately outside Vila Real.
To return: Walk to Castro Marim and, from there, return by taxi for your bus or train (Timetables 8, 9) from Vila Real to Faro. Or by 🚗

Some 20 minutes into the walk you can see familiar farmland crops just a short distance away — very different from the vegetation growing close to the salinas, *where only salt-tolerant plants like the glassworts* (Arthrocnemem sp) *and the saltworts* (Salicornia sp) *can survive.*

Shorter walk: to the salt plant and return (9.8km/6.1mi; 1h45min; easy). Follow the main walk as far as the locked gate (not far past the salt plant; 53min) and return the same way. This avoids the more difficult path near the end of the walk, while still seeing the best of the reserve.

Although the walk starts just to the south of Castro Marim, it is well worth having a look around the town — either before you start out or at the end of the walk. If you are travelling by public transport, save this until the end of the walk, so that you can take a taxi back from there to Vila Real. A castle and a 17th-century fort dominate the town. The castle is believed to have its origins back in Roman times, but was the seat of the Knights of Christ in the 14th century until this was transferred to Tomar. The earthquake of 1755 largely destroyed the castle, although parts still remain, and the present castle was built by King Afonso III. You can stroll around inside to inspect the old walls and enjoy its commanding location, looking over the Rio Guadiana towards Ayamonte in Spain.

The nature reserve itself covers the area of *salinas* south and east of the town. *Salinas* are the production units used to obtain sea salt. They are flooded with sea water which is allowed to evaporate under the influence of the sun and the strong coastal winds, until the salt finally crystallises out. With its long hot summers, Algarve is an ideal location for salt production by this method, and its history dates back more than 2500 years, from the time when salt was first produced for preserving fish. Castro Marim was a particularly important centre for this activity, and a 1791 survey revealed that there were 185 active *salinas* in this region alone. They are vastly reduced in numbers now, but those that remain are valuable sites for wild life, especially for wading birds and waterfowl. This walk will delight the bird-watchers particularly, and the birds that you can expect to see, depending on the season, include flamingos, *Phoenicopterus ruber*, in a large flock, the lovely black-winged stilt, *Himantopus himantopus*, which is the symbol of this reserve, the white stork, *Ciconia ciconia*, and a variety of other birds which we are not skilled enough to identify. The list of known visitors to the reserve is too long to quote in full, but includes a number of sandpipers such as the

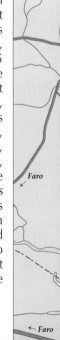

Faro

← Faro

dunlin, *Calidris alpina,* plovers like the ringed plover, *Charadrius hiaticula*, and the avocet, *Recurvirostra avosetta.*

The route described is the *only* circuit in the reserve; it is not possible to short-cut the circuit by using the banks that divide the *salinas.* Any attempt to do this may be dangerous and will result in you retracing your steps.

Start the walk from the N122 just south of **Castro Marim** (22 minutes' walking from the centre) and 1.6km/ 1mi north of the N125. Take the track heading west, where cultivation south of Castro Marim ends. A ruined building on the left is passed in **3min**, as you head out towards the *salinas.* From here the river over to the left becomes more noticeable. At the point where the course of the river swings away to the left (**11min**), note that the path on the left is the return route. Olive and carob groves on the right add colour and contrast to the flatness of the *salinas* now on the left. The flamingos are usually in a large flock, so they are easily seen across the emptiness of the large lagoons. Stay with the main track, as you swing around right, to get good views of Castro Marim. The closest point to the castle is reached in **24min**, as you swing left on meeting the river. Keep following the main track, with an eye open for the wading birds in some of the shallower parts of the reserve. As the sun gets stronger

The flock of flamingos is often seen at these large salinas near the start of the walk. If they are too frequently disturbed by visitors, they move to the quieter western parts of the reserve. No matter where they are, if you complete the circuit, you should see them at some point.

the storks take to the wing, and they can be seen lazily circling and rising on the thermals.

The SALT PLANT is reached in **42min** and is on the left. In **53min** reach a crossing track with a LOCKED GATE *(where the Shorter walk returns).*Climb over the gate or the adjacent wall, or go round the wall via the ditch. (The reserve is private property, and the owners tolerate walkers but not vehicular traffic.)

From here the track winds between dykes. Vila Real fills the skyline ahead for a time but, as you swing left, Castro Marim comes back into view. Follow the track to a white PUMPING STATION (**1h32min**). Here turn left, along the top of a DYKE, with the river close by on the right, and the railway just over the river. For a time you might wonder if you are on the right route, since the path level has been raised by dredging. This is being trampled down, but it has made for some tricky walking in places. Again, you might wonder, when you see the very good track running parallel on the next embankment to the left … but rest assured that, if you stay by the riverside, this path connects up with your outward route.

Keep following the banks of the river, taking the line of least resistance. Note that, in **1h55min**, the good track over on the left swings away to head towards the salt plant, whereas our path meets a broad path two minutes later, where you turn right to head back to the outward track. A sharp right turn, when you meet the track (**2h 04min**), leads you back to the N122 (**2h15min**).

BUS AND TRAIN TIMETABLES

Eva Transportes (www.eva-bus.com) operates local buses all over Algarve as well as servicing long distance routes to Lisbon, Porto and many other major towns throughout Portugal. Its colourful yellow, green and blue logo, along with the word Eva, is used to mark the buses and the bus stops. Froto Azul, a smaller bus company, operates services out of Portimão to Monchique and a joint service with Eva to Silves. Printed timetables often can be obtained on request at the main bus stations, but demand usually exceeds supply. At least the timetables are posted at the main bus stations and at tourist offices, so it pays to have pen and paper handy to note down a few times.

Remember that bus timetables are liable to change without notice, so always be sure to check the times of your bus. Do not rely solely on the timetables printed on the following pages. Buses are not numbered, but the final destination is displayed on the front, so be sure to check before you board.

For some bus journeys it is necessary to book a ticket before you board, particularly when you board at a bus station; for others you pay on the bus. On some journeys there is a 15 per cent discount if you book a return ticket. If you are setting out on a long-distance journey, it is normal to book in advance. If your accommodation is not near a bus station, you can book through a nearby travel agency. The tourist office will advise you of the nearest.

In the list below, the numbers following place names refer to **bus timetable numbers** (except for 9, which is a **train timetable**). The train is considerably cheaper than the bus but, be warned, it is often much slower.

Albufeira 5, 7, 9	Monchique 3
Albufeira station 9	Paderne 7
Burgau 1	Portimão 3, 4, 9
Caldas de Monchique 3	Sagres 2
Estói 6	Salema 2
Faro 6, 8, 9	São Brás de Alportel 6
Figueira 2	Silves 4, 5, 9
Lagoa 4, 9	Tavira 8, 9
Lagos 1, 2, 9	Vila Real de SA 8, 9
Luz 1	

Timetables begin on the next page.

1 Lagos — Luz — Burgau

Daily departures
Journey times: Lagos — Luz 15min; Lagos — Burgau 22min
Departs Lagos 06.55a; 09.00; 09.45b; 11.15; 13.05; 14.55; 16.35;
    18.20; 19.25
Departs Burgau 07.33a; 09.48; 10.08b; 11.59; 14.28; 15.48;
    17.03; 17.16; 19.03
a = except Sundays; b = Sundays only

2 Lagos — Salema — Figueira — Sagres

Daily departures
Journey times: Lagos — Salema 32min, Lagos — Sagres 1h05min
Departs Lagos 09.10; 10.50; 15.00; 18.00; 18.30a; 19.30a; 20.35
Departs Sagres 07.40; 08.20b; 12.05; 17.20c; 18.25a; 19.10;
    19.35a
a = daily in summer but not Saturdays or Sundays between 16 September
    and 30 June
b = except Sundays and holidays
c = not Saturdays or Sundays

3 Portimão — Monchique

Daily departure times

Portimão (depart)	09.00, 10.00, 11.15, 14.15, 17.15, 18.15, 19.30
Caldas de Monchique*	~~00.00~~, ~~00.00~~, ~~00.00~~, 14.45, ~~00.00~~, ~~00.00~~, 20.02
Monchique (arrive)	09.32, 10.32, 11.47, 15.00, 18.00, 18.47, 20.17
Monchique (depart)	07.00, 08.00, 10.00, 12.30, 14.00, 15.30, 18.15
Caldas de Monchique*	07.16, ~~00.00~~, ~~00.00~~, ~~00.00~~, 14.16, 15.46, ~~00.00~~
Portimão (arrive)	07.45, 08.45, 10.38, 13.08, 14.45, 16.15, 18.53

~~00.00~~ = does not call
*The bus stops on the main road above Caldas, leaving a short walk down to
the village

4 Portimão — Lagoa — Silves

Daily departures
Journey time Portimão — Lagoa 20min, Portimão — Silves 35min
Departs Portimão 08.30a; 08.55; 09.35; 10.45a: 11.30a; 12.00;
    13.10a; 13.30a; 14.00; 14.30a; 15.50; 17.456; 18.35a; 19.10
Departs Silves 07.20a; 07.25a; 08.05; 08.20a; 09.00; 10.30;
    11.05; 13.20a; 14.20a; 15.00a; 16.30a; 18.00
a = except Saturdays and Sundays

5 Albufeira — Silves

Daily departures
Journey time Albufeira — Silves 42min
Departs Albufeira 07.30b; 08.30a; 09.45b; 12.35; 14.15; 17.15b;
    17.25a; 18.45
Departs Silves 06.43; 07.48c; 09.00b; 10.30b; 13.30; 16.30b;
    18.00
a = daily in summer but not Saturdays or Sundays between 16 September
    and 30 June
b = daily in summer but not Sundays between 16 September and 30 June
c = except Saturdays and Sundays

6 Faro — Estói — São Brás

Departure times (weekdays)

Faro	Estói	São Brás de Alportel		Estói	Faro
		arrive	depart		
07.45	08.05	08.20	07.00	07.21	07.42
09.00	09.15a	09.27	07.10	07.20a	07.38
10.15	10.35	10.50	00.00	07.25	07.43
12.10	12.36	12.50	08.15	08.25a	08.43
12.35	12.57	00.00	00.00	08.25	08.47
13.35	13.55	14.10	09.50	10.05	10.25
16.30	16.50	17.05	12.35	12.50	13.10
17.30	17.48	17.58	00.00	13.00	13.22
18.25	18.47	19.08	00.00	13.30	13.48
18.30	18.50	19.05	14.15	14.30	14.50
18.40	18.58	00.00	15.20	15.35	15.55
19.15	19.37	00.00	17.30	17.45	18.05
19.20	19.39a	19.50	00.00	18.15	18.35
			18.45	19.00	19.20

Departure times (weekends)

Faro	Estói	São Brás de Alportel		Estói	Faro
07.45b	08.05b	08.20	00.00	07.25	07.45
09.00	09.25	09.27	07.10	07.26a	07.45
12.35	12.51	13.06	09.50c	10.05b	10.25
13.35	13.57	14.10	00.00	13.00a	13.22
16.30	16.50	17.05	14.15b	14.30	14.50
18.25	18.47	19.08	17.30	17.45	18.05
19.20	19.39a	19.50	19.30c	19.40a	20.05

a = bus does not enter Estói, but stops at the crossroads about 1km away — convenient both for visiting the Roman ruins (Milreu) and for Walk 17
b = Saturdays only
c = Sundays only
00.00 = does not call

7 Albufeira — Paderne

Daily departures
Journey time Albufeira — Paderne 21min
Departs Albufeira 07.50a; 09.25a. 12.05b; 13.40; 16.45b; 17.40; 18.35; 19.30
Departs Paderne 07.10a; 08.02a; 09.50b; 12.35b; 18.14b; 18.40b
a = except Saturdays and Sundays
b = except Saturdays, Sundays and holidays

8 Faro — Tavira — Vila Real de Santo António

Daily departures
Journey times: Faro — Tavira 1h, Faro — Vila Real 1h40min
Departs Faro 7.15; 8.00a; 9.00; 11.00; 12.15a; 13.25, 15.15; 16.35; 17.40a; 18.20; 19.30
Departs Vila Real 7.05; 8.15b; 10.00; 11.20; 12.15; 14.30; 16.30; 17.30a; 18.30
a = except Saturdays, Sundays and national holidays
b = except Sundays

9 Train timetable, Lagos — Vila Real

This is an extract from the full timetable which is extensive and available free of charge from most railway stations and some tourist offices. All the train departures are listed below, but only a selection of stations is included. *Note that over-65s can get a 50% discount on fares on production of a passport as proof of age.*

Lagos	Portimão	Silves	Albufeira	Faro	Tavira	V Real
~~00.00~~	~~00.00~~	~~00.00~~	05.21	06.15	07.05	07.44
~~00.00~~	~~00.00~~	~~00.00~~	07.03	08.00	08.52	09.37
06.10	06.40	06.59	07.47	08.30	~~00.00~~	~~00.00~~
07.15	07.31	07.45	08.16	08.55	09.29	09.54
07.55	08.29	08.48	09.23	10.10	~~00.00~~	~~00.00~~
09.33	09.57	10.13	10.46	~~00.00~~	~~00.00~~	~~00.00~~
~~00.00~~	~~00.00~~	~~00.00~~	~~00.00~~	10.15	11.04	11.48
~~00.00~~	~~00.00~~	~~00.00~~	~~00.00~~	12.12	13.00	~~00.00~~
~~00.00~~	~~00.00~~	~~00.00~~	12.31	13.02	13.38	14.07
12.15	12.33	12.49	13.19	~~00.00~~	~~00.00~~	~~00.00~~
13.30	13.52	14.14	~~00.00~~	~~00.00~~	~~00.00~~	~~00.00~~
~~00.00~~	~~00.00~~	~~00.00~~	15.03	16.03	16.50	17.40
14.15	14.48	15.09	15.49	16.45	~~00.00~~	~~00.00~~
18.20	18.36	18.50	19.25	19.56	20.30	20.55
19.12	19.42	20.06	20.49	21.35	22.17	22.53

V Real	Tavira	Faro	Albufeira	Silves	Portimão	Lagos
05.30	06.03	06.45	07.27	08.12	08.30	08.53
06.35	07.09	07.52	08.33	~~00.00~~	~~00.00~~	~~00.00~~
07.50	08.17	08.57	09.24	09.47	09.59	10.15
08.55	09.31	10.25	11.11	12.09	12.32	12.59
10.20	11.05	11.51	~~00.00~~	~~00.00~~	~~00.00~~	~~00.00~~
~~00.00~~	~~00.00~~	12.20	13.18	13.55	14.19	14.44
12.40	13.07	13.46	~~00.00~~	~~00.00~~	~~00.00~~	~~00.00~~
14.20	15.00	15.53	16.49	~~00.00~~	~~00.00~~	~~00.00~~
16.15	16.49	17.30	17.57	~~00.00~~	~~00.00~~	~~00.00~~
~~00.00~~	~~00.00~~	17.45	18.38	19.19	19.40	20.07
16.55	17.43	18.35	~~00.00~~	~~00.00~~	~~00.00~~	~~00.00~~
17.55	18.26	19.06	19.40	20.08	20.16	20.30
19.05	19.54	20.50	21.36	~~00.00~~	~~00.00~~	~~00.00~~
21.40	22.16	23.00	23.35			

~~00.00~~ = does not call

10 Bus services: Lagoa — Benagil; Magoa — Praia da Marinha

Daily departures
Departs Lagoa 9.25; arrives Benagil 9.40
Departs Lagoa 15.00; arrives Benagil 15.15
Departs Lagoa 08.50; arrives Praia da Marinha 09.05
Departs Lagoa 14.20; arrives Praia da Marinha 14.35
This is a new service found on www.eva-bus.com. Return times were not shown. The web site also indicates a new service from Lagoa to Armação de Pera.

● Index

Geographical names comprise the only entries in this index. For subject entries, see Contents, page 3. *Italic type* indicates a map reference; **bold face type** a photograph. Both of these may be in addition to a text reference on the same page.

STOP PRESS: BORDEIRA CIRCUIT

This walk is shown on a board in a large lay-by opposite the road into Bordeira off the N268 north of Vila do Bispo. The route leads through a valley once filled with paddy fields. Yes! Algarve was once a rice-growing area. The concrete towers, spread at intervals along the main track through the valley, appear to have been sluice gates to control the water flow. You rise through *matos*-covered hills to the high point at the hamlet of Monte Novo, then relish magnificent views along the west coast on the return.

Distance: 15km/9.4mi; 3h15min

Grade: moderate; all on tracks. After an initial short uphill section near the start, there is a gradual rise from the 35min-point to the hamlet of Monte Novo, the half-way point. Beyond Monte Novo, two short stretches of woodland *provide the only shade en route.* Four information boards provide good markers along the way; the first is in the lay-by at the start. The only opportunity for refreshments is in Bordeira (worth a look) or nearby Carrapateira. Monte Novo is only a small hamlet, so carry water and a picnic with you. *Note: Don't rely on any of the boards being in place!*

How to get there: 🚌 Park in the large lay-by opposite the road entrance to Bordeira on the N268 along the west coast.

Start out in the lay-by, by BOARD NO 1. Head northwest down the track out of the lay-by, opposite the Bordeira road. In under a minute, fork right to cross a concrete ford. Turn left uphill at the track junction (**5min**) then downhill right, into the valley, at the next junction (**14min**). If the deep pool, where a winter stream crosses, is full of water, stay on the right-hand side and cross on some stones sunk into the mud. When you meet a crossing track by a CONCRETE TOWER with iron rungs on the left (**28min**), turn right. *(The Short circuit for motorists goes left here.)*

At the T-junction (**34min**) turn left, to reach BOARD NO 2 a minute later. Rise in the direction of Monte Novo, and keep left on the main track where another track continues ahead to the farmhouse at MONTE VELHO (**1h07min**). Pass an isolated building on the left and continue to the BOARD NO 3 at the entrance to **Monte Novo**. Wend your way through the hamlet to the left, ignoring side-tracks. The road reverts to track, and views open up along the west coast.

A gradual descent leads south to BOARD NO 4 (**2h09min**), where a track leads right to a trig point. Descend to a 5-WAY JUNCTION, with a large threshing floor on the left, possibly used for rice and cereals. *(The Short circuit for motorists enters from the left here.)* Stay ahead, skirting to the left of farm buildings up to the right (**2h46min**) and passing two smaller threshing floors. At a staggered junction (**3h**), keep round to the left. Cross a ford over a river, and ignore a track off to the right. Your track keeps ahead, skirting fields on the left, and takes you back to the lay-by at BOARD NO 1.

Short Borderira circuit for motorists (5.8km/3.6mi; 1h13min). Easy-moderate. Follow the notes above to the 28min-point and turn left. In 15min you reach the 5-way junction (the 2h46min-point in the main walk). Turn left here, back to the start of the walk.

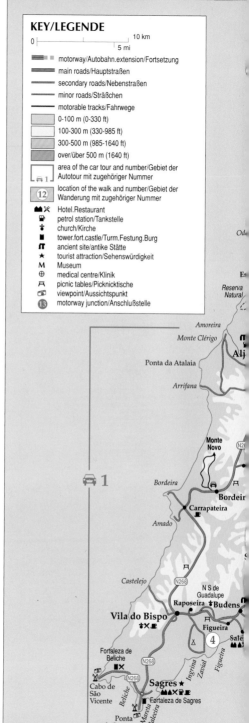

KEY/LEGENDE

0	10 km
	5 mi

▬▬ ▪ motorway/Autobahn.extension/Fortsetzung
▬▬ main roads/Hauptstraßen
▬▬ secondary roads/Nebenstraßen
▬▬ minor roads/Sträßchen
▬▬ motorable tracks/Fahrwege

☐ 0-100 m (0-330 ft)
☐ 100-300 m (330-985 ft)
☐ 300-500 m (985-1640 ft)
☐ over/über 500 m (1640 ft)

🚗1 area of the car tour and number/Gebiet der Autotour mit zugehöriger Nummer
12 location of the walk and number/Gebiet der Wanderung mit zugehöriger Nummer

🏨✖ Hotel.Restaurant
⛽ petrol station/Tankstelle
⛪ church/Kirche
🏰 tower.fort.castle/Turm.Festung.Burg
⛩ ancient site/antike Stätte
★ tourist attraction/Sehenswürdigkeit
M Museum
⊕ medical centre/Klinik
🅿 picnic tables/Picknicktische
📷 viewpoint/Aussichtspunkt
13 motorway junction/Anschlußstelle

Ode

Es
Reserva
Natural

Amoreira
Monte Clérigo
Ponta da Atalaia
Arrifana
Alj

🚗1

Monte
Novo (N2

Bordeira
Carrapateira
Amado
Bordeir

Castelejo (N268)

N S de
Guadalupe
Raposeira ⛪Budens
Vila do Bispo
⛪✖🅿
Figueira
Sale

Fortaleza de
Beliche
🏰✖
Cabo de
São
Vicente
Beliche (N268)
(N268)
Sagres ★
🏨🏰✖⛽🅿
Fortaleza de Sagres
Ponta
de Sagres

Bras de Portel ↑
21

Avenida de Olivença

15

Leão Penedo

16

Farense

Rua de São Luís

Avenida de Olivença

Dr Jeronimo Costa de Moura

Dr Joaquim Osorio

Praceta Coronel
Pires Viegras
13

General Theofilo Trinidad

Brito Cabrera

General Humberto Delgado

Cruz dos Mestres

João de Deus

Dr Candido

Guedes

Eça de Quieroz

Dr Teixeira

Guerreiro

Avenida 5 de Outubro

Avenida 5 de Outubro

Dr Justino Crimano

Pedro Nunes

Dr José de Matos

Vasco da Gama

18

Praça da
Liberdade **1**

8

Sto António

9

Pé da Cruz

Rebelo da Silva

Rua Castilho

Rua do Bocage

Rua da Polícia de Segurança Publica

Almadeda
João de Deus
12

3

Dias

17

9

Largo de
São Francisco

Estrada do Cais Comercial

5

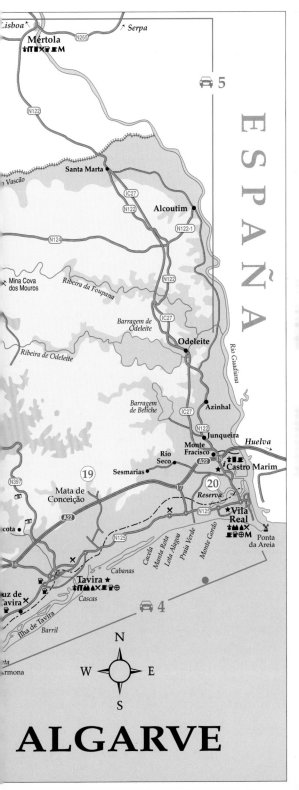

ALGARVE

FARO

1 Tourist information/Tourist-
   Information
2 Main square/Hauptplatz
3 Police/Polizei
4 TAP offices/Tap-Büro
5 Port/Hafen

6 Marina/Jachthafe
7 Telephones/Telefo
8 Bank area/Banke
9 Museums/Musee
10 Bus station/Busba
11 Tank rank/Taxiha
12 Parks

N125, Vila Real, Espanha →

Rua de Berlim

Ataíde de

9

Praça do
Infante

Olivença

Rua de Berlim

Avezedo Coutinho

Caldas Xavier

do Bom João

Moinho da Palmeira

...way station/Bahnhof

...ter tower (near the road to
...Bras)/Wasserturm (nahe der
...ße nach São Bras)